W9-AUX-694

Broken Glass

Broken
GLASS

A Family's Journey
Through Mental Illness

ROBERT V. HINE

University of New Mexico Press
ALBUQUERQUE

YEAR   PRINTING
10 09 08 07 06   1 2 3 4 5

Library of Congress Cataloging-in-Publication Data

Hine, Robert V., 1921–
  Broken glass : a family's journey through mental illness / Robert V.
Hine.
     p. cm.
  ISBN-13: 978-0-8263-3997-3 (pbk. : alk. paper)
  ISBN-10: 0-8263-3997-2 (pbk. : alk. paper)
  1. Hine, Elene—Mental health. 2. Schizophrenics—California—
Biography. 3. Schizophrenics—California—Family relations. I. Title.
  RC514.H36 2006
  616.89'80092—dc22

                    2006004713

                    Book design and composition by Damien Shay
                              Body type is Utopia 10/14
                        Display is Washout and Utopia Bold

For two brave women

Contents

Preface

Among the readers of this book I assume there will be parents of mentally disturbed offspring. To them I extend my hand. I cannot give them a treatise of how and why. E. Fuller Torrey and Michael Foster Green are among the many who can helpfully guide them through the science. Instead I offer no more than a highly personal account that I assume will resonate in at least some of its particulars. If it does, I will consider the job worth doing.

Alas, parents and patients are not alone. Mental illness does affect so many of us—directly as siblings, teachers, and health-care workers and indirectly as friends and citizens watching the homeless roam our streets. If we open our eyes, we are surrounded by its ravages, and my story is one small island in a stormy archipelago.

Not that I have written it alone. So many of the details are drawn from my wife's memory, bless her. And my daughter has given me permission to go ahead with the effort. I have not asked her to read it yet, however, because I know she would react quite differently to many of the events I describe. Where I felt sadness and dejection, she very likely felt release and exultation. Where I felt helplessness, she very likely felt in happy control. Where I saw confusion and delusion, she may well have seen purpose and steadiness. This is not the story she would tell, especially since I have changed many names to preserve privacy. It is solely mine, solely the viewpoint of one man, solely a father's feelings about his daughter.

The dedication of this book only begins to express my appreciation for my wife and daughter. My brother, Richard Hine, and my sister, Katherine Shaha, have, as always, supported and urged me in the writing. Many friends, such as Don Stoutenborough and Edgar Montoya, encouraged me. Karen Lystra offered wonderful suggestions. My editors, Elizabeth Hadas and Valerie Larkin, provided superb criticism. Elizabeth Hadas deserves special thanks, not only for editing, but also for gently steering the manuscript through earlier versions. May they all accept my warmest gratitude.

My deepest wish is that the parents of the mentally ill will find here consolation in the life they lead and encouragement in holding the course, however trying it may sometimes seem. For them and others I only hope that I lift a lamp beside that double locked door.

Chapter One

Prelude at Planter's Dock

Shirley and I had our own window over the bay as we sat in a booth at Planter's Dock in Oakland. Shirley's hair was in its usual pageboy. It struck me as pure poetry, sensuous and gorged with feeling. My eyes kept catching bits of candlelight reflected in its gold. No one sat near us. The restaurant was dense with Asian color like Tiffany glass. The whole scene was insufferably romantic, exactly the way I wanted it.

I intended to ask the big question tonight, and it finally came with the dessert of green-tea ice cream.

"I want us to get married. Will you marry me?"

Her eyes were down, but soon she looked straight into mine. "I was hoping it would be tonight."

We started reviewing prospects. I had a graduate school fellowship and was close to my Ph.D. She had a job and would be happy to keep it. But she seemed distracted. Had I said something wrong? She was looking out to the dark sea, not at me. The fog, coming in fast, brushed against the windows as if trying to listen.

"You don't know enough about me," she said.

"I know all I need to know."

"No. You don't."

"Is there a million dollars you haven't told me about?"

"I'm serious, Robert. I can't say yes or no 'til I tell you all of this." She seemed to be feeding on my eyes, and in hers I saw flecks of pain. "If we marry, we shouldn't ever have children." She

1

stopped. I tried to fathom what she had said. Her sentence did not die; it was erect on the table between us, standing on its own feet, brazenly unwilling to dissolve into an echo. I picked up my wine glass and then put it down again without drinking.

I didn't know what to say. I just looked at her as she went on. "My father is a hemophiliac. I carry the bleeder's genes."

My napkin was wadded into a ball.

She looked away from me as if talking to herself. "It's more than a disease. It's a curse. It's a curse on what a boy wants to do, must do, rough and tumble. A bruise eventually engulfs his whole arm. A break is a major disaster. He has appendicitis and the surgeon dreads to operate. When he starts to shave, every nick is jeopardy. You know it's only a disease for males?"

Somehow I got out a dumb question. "How does that work?"

"Women are the carriers. That's why I can't give you children or I wouldn't want us to have children. I have to see that it's stopped, at least on one of its journeys." I thought she was going to cry.

I must have seemed insensitive because I said nothing. I thought of my mother and how she dreamed of showing Europe to her grandchildren.

On a different level I heard myself saying, "There are far worse problems than hemophilia. Maybe there'll soon be cures—serums. To make blood coagulate doesn't sound so difficult to me."

"I don't want us to take that chance."

I asked, "How do you feel about adoption?"

"How do *you* feel about it?"

"We could choose the sex. Even the race."

"How would you choose?"

"I don't know."

In the dim light of the candles I could see tears forming in Shirley's eyes. I wanted to hug her, but instead I held her hand and blurted out, "We can adopt, we know that. But listen, love, you're not the only one with problems. You certainly remember the ones you're getting with me."

My thoughts were suddenly clogged with lying in bed motionless all during my seventeenth year, every joint struggling with juvenile rheumatoid arthritis. Like a montage I caught the pain of breaking the joints back into use. There had followed an eye disease that had grown out of the arthritis and proved resistant to medication. But I had recovered enough to resume college, and there I had met Shirley. We were close enough friends that she knew that my eyes remained vulnerable.

So my own montage of problems flashed on the mental screen, and I wondered why Shirley would ever choose me. How had I been so crazy as to even ask? Yet here she was making an impediment of her own.

My eyes must have been glistening, too, because I couldn't see her shining hair now, and I wanted to see it. I kept blinking. "We've got plenty of reasons to adopt, and they aren't all yours."

Then I leaned far over the table and pulled her hand close. "Remember, children or no children, I want to marry you. Please, will you marry me?"

I could feel the options narrow. We were in love. We were twenty-eight and twenty-nine years old. My near doctorate and her good job said we had lots going for us.

I think she was counting off the options, too, because I could see her begin to nod. I moved over to her side of the booth and hugged her. I wanted to squeeze all those tears out of her eyes. I wanted her to squeeze out mine. I wanted to sail out into that fog and keep Shirley warm as we went. We knew what we were doing and we were happy.

Chapter Two

Orange Groves

In 1954 we had been married for five years and we lived in Riverside, southern California. After a year of renting, we built our own house. How I loved that house—not big, two bedrooms, one story with a barn roof of shakes, exterior of gray bat-and-board, a long screened porch facing rows of Riverside Navel orange trees, whose blossoms drenched the spring air. The house reinforced our idiosyncrasies—a kitchen area for Shirley's full-size loom; built-in, see-through book shelves as room dividers; a living room alcove for my grandmother's carved, black, upright Knabe with chipped yellow keys and a tone that rivaled angels. The living room was dominated by a rough stone fireplace.

Our married life had included a couple of years in New Haven, where I studied at Yale and we lived poor, sharing the upstairs of a rattletrap house with a Polish woman in a run-down neighborhood near the harbor. We moved to Pasadena to take my first job, a fellowship at the nearby Huntington Library ($3,000 a year, a princely sum). After studying utopian colonies for two years, I accepted an instructorship at the new Riverside college of the University of California ($4,100 a year), and we built our dream house.

It was time to think about adoption. Sex for us had been good. But we were always careful, wholly committed to blocking the spread of hemophilia. Shirley used a diaphragm, and she became skillful in getting it in quickly, wherever we were. More than once I offered to use a condom, but she said no, this was fine.

We began to talk about adoption over dinner or in bed at night. The lights-out talks were the best. Fingers of doubt reached further in the darkness, and questions rattled around in the dark corners. We might know something about the mother, but what about the father? What if we got a child whose genetic imprint was wrong for us?

Shirley always believed nurture to be the most important thing. "Whatever our child is, we'll love it into shape."

Maelstroms of worry inevitably swirled. We don't need a child. Plenty of couples are childless, happy enough with one another. But we always came back to the feeling that our good fortune only meant we have much to share. We wanted a child.

Shirley's parents had had good experiences with adoptions and were supportive. Mine were a bit more circumspect. When we told them we were thinking of adoption, my father smiled weakly. My mother stared with ever so slight a frown. My aunt, who lived with them, said "Oh," not quite a plea, not quite a resignation. After an all-thumbs silence, my mother said, "Have you thought of the dangers?"

But we got their ambiguous blessings, and we set in. First step was the Children's Home Society of Los Angeles. For them we filled out reams of applications, preliminaries to their investigations of our backgrounds, our finances, our health records.

We put down a girl as our preference and felt pretty confident. I had a good job (assistant professor, tenure track, in the University of California). Shirley planned to give up her job (an arts secretary on the campus) when we had the baby. We were settled, owning our house without too big a mortgage.

Our home visitation was arranged for a Sunday morning in early December. We were up before six and ate our cereal and banana fast, pulling apart the Sunday *Times* half-heartedly, then stacking it neatly on the coffee table in the living room. Shirley had brought the house to a shine yesterday, and now we quickly washed the dishes, made the bed, and saw that everything was in its place. I wore a pullover sweater with a sport shirt, Shirley a plain skirt and flowered blouse.

Promptly at ten the bell rang and we opened the door to a rotund man and a tall woman with horn-rimmed glasses. We gave them coffee in our best wedding-present set.

The woman opened her notebook and began. "So you want to adopt a child. Why?"

I was happy to let Shirley start. "We want children and we can't have them on our own."

I cringed inside a bit at the plural—children. We hadn't talked about more than one.

"I haven't seen anything in your medical records to indicate you can't have natural children."

"No," Shirley said shakily, "it's a personal thing. We want to avoid my family's history of hemophilia. I explained that to the people in Los Angeles."

"So as far as you know you could have children naturally?"

I thought I had better say something. "As far as we know. But we are very careful."

"I understand," said the woman.

We've lost the first round, I thought.

She went on unfazed. "How do you feel about raising children? What will you do when they misbehave? Have you read Benjamin Spock?"

Shirley and I looked at each other. That was a whopper. I certainly didn't want to take that one, so I just smiled at Shirley and she stepped in. "Yes. I know Spock. In general I like his ideas. I want to give a child room to develop."

That worried me. So I said, "We understand though that you can overdo that one." Then it occurred to me that we didn't want to give the impression that we argued over such things. So I added, "Of course, Shirley's right basically."

They were there for close to two hours. As they left, the woman warned us that the society had six families waiting for every available white child. It was like pouring sand on our hopes. But we thanked them profusely and they left.

When we sank on the couch together, all I could feel was my armpits still dripping inside my shirt. "We blew that one," I said.

"What do you mean? I think we did fine."

"Look at this house," I went on. "Look at that neatly folded newspaper. Look at every dish in its place in the kitchen. Look at the towels, each folded carefully. How could you raise a kid in this environment? I'll bet they thought that way."

"Oh, nonsense. They know everyone puts on a good front. That only makes us normal. Besides, we are orderly. What's wrong with raising a child to be orderly?"

"I'll bet they pegged me as a cold, fuddy-duddy scholar."

"You're impossible. We did fine. Hold that thought."

Why, we never knew, but I was right. We were turned down. The letter was warm and friendly, explaining that there was at the moment a shortage of white children available for adoption and the society was forced to make difficult choices.

"I think we should have left the paper strewn around," I said to Shirley. Somewhere deep within me was a glimmer of relief. I wasn't at all sure about me as a father. "Maybe they were right," I said. "Maybe we wouldn't make good parents."

We nursed our rejection for a few months. One of our friends was appalled at the decision. She knew a psychologist who worked as a counselor with an obstetrician. They occasionally had patients who opted to give birth but not keep the child. For them the doctor arranged private adoptions, the legal work for which was handled by the Los Angeles County Bureau of Adoptions. The counselor sought good adoptive parents; the obstetrician in a sense provided the child.

The counselor gave us a battery of psychological and behavioral tests. We met with the doctor. We agreed to pay the doctor's fees and the hospital bills, but nothing else that might suggest an illegal exchange of money. Eventually the doctor assured us that we had passed all the barriers. All we needed to do was wait for a baby to become available.

That summer they informed us that a baby was expected in late December, and if the birth went well, it could be ours. We were floating downstream in a roiling current, breathing pure joy, catching the same breath in fear.

We were not permitted to talk with the mother, but we had the option of allowing a lawyer to do so. I called our friend Don, who had just set up his first law practice. He arranged to call on the young mother, now at her parents' home in San

Marino. He had a long talk with her, and then drove straight out to Riverside.

His first words were, "I'd say all systems are go."

He went on to describe the young woman as healthy, rather nice looking, dark brown hair, and hazel eyes, a student at Pasadena City College, where she was interested in the arts. The baby's father, also a student at the college, did not know about his offspring.

I remember feeling weights peeling off my back one by one.

Don stayed for supper, and by the time we finished we were jabbering freely about the young mother with her hazel eyes and dark brown hair and vivacious manner. We toasted her in cabernet. I could see her in my mind's eye. What would be her relation to us? We'd never meet her, of course; that was one of the rules that had been laid down. She would be a lone spirit wandering outside the realm of motherhood while Shirley took on her abandoned role as mother. And I would assume the position of father, substituting for that errant young man who would never know what marks he had made in the sand.

The call from the doctor came in late November. The baby had been born two weeks early. It was a girl, and she was at St. Luke's Hospital in Altadena. We could come over anytime and see the baby, but not the mother. We wasted no time.

Oh, when we saw that child! She was beautiful, with tiny ears and a bit of blonde hair, no wrinkled face, no redness, a dream child, and ours! The fears all evaporated. Our blood hummed sweetly, and our hearts pumped full of cool joy. In three days we could take her home!

The obstetrician advised that we have a pediatrician of our choice examine the baby. We hired one from the Riverside Clinic and he reported a breach birth and a completely healthy, normal child.

Three days of scurry. Shirley resigned her job, and her committee gave us a silver baby dish, the first tangible recognition of our impending transformed life. It had a little handle that provided our first intimation of a tiny hand. We bought diapers, bassinet, bottles—growing piles of tactile evidence.

And we discussed names. But that didn't take us long. We were both hopeless romantics, and when we hit upon Elene, we chimed back and forth with allusions. Shirley saw "Elaine the fair, Elaine the lovable, Elaine the lily maid of Astolat," and I saw "the face that launched a thousand ships and burnt the topless towers of Ilium." We would pronounce her name Elaine but the spelling would be Elene, which would suggest Helen of Troy as well. So with the rousing approval of all the Knights of the Round Table, Prince Paris, and even his mother Hecuba, we named our newborn child Elene.

When Elene was three days old, we drove to Altadena and brought her to our dream house in the orange groves of Riverside. The first night the baby slept in a crib on Shirley's side of the bed. The two of them fell asleep fairly quickly. I lay awake. An owl hooted. Owls were unusual in Riverside. I was superstitious enough to not like hooting owls. Did the wise old bird not approve what we had done? Suddenly I thought of Elene's natural mother. She had had three days with that beautiful baby. How could she have gone through with it? She would have a few months, of course, to change her mind. Was she crying herself to sleep tonight? We could have lived a good life without babies. If Elene's mother decided to take her back, we could still do that.

No, I don't hope she takes Elene back. I don't. Our signatures on those papers were solemn vows. In effect we had pledged to love, honor, cherish, and protect this little life, until death do us part. And when the owl hooted again, I said, almost aloud, "Get on with it. You've got the wrong house. We here are at peace, overflowing with peace. Go sing your dark questioning somewhere else."

Chapter Three

Lurking Presence

Elene was a Dr. Spock baby. In addition she was a Mozart baby. Shirley rocked her and fed her to classical music. Our friends said Elene was weaned on Mozart. There are theories that classical music, Mozart in particular, will build better brains. If true, Elene's brain cells were summarily and abundantly nourished.

Elene as a baby was a delight. We were thrilled when she talked early, but we were a bit puzzled by her first words, "Mama coming." They became her baby mantra underscoring how hard it was for her to be separated from Shirley. She would toddle from room to room saying "Mama coming," as if she knew she had once been separated from a mother and she wasn't going to let it happen again.

But she exuded joy and seemed to smile at life. I have a picture of her when she had three upper teeth and two below, leaning on a bed, holding up a sock of mine, her eyes half closed, laughing as if it were the funniest thing in the world.

She did have some problems, though. At a very early age, maybe two, she had difficulty accepting presents. At her second birthday party, she opened one package, and then something seemed to snap. She fell apart. She cried. She fell down, crying hard. "I don't want any presents." She was inconsolable. Some lurking presence, some hidden threat in those presents seemed to frighten her, or something about the uncertainty of unrevealed contents unsettled her. The other kids looked on in amazement.

Elene ran to her room crying. Shirley followed. The other parents rose and I bid them farewell, and there were expressed sympathies and presumed understandings. When they were all gone, I stood there alone for a moment, listening to Elene still crying loudly in her room, and I knew Shirley was holding her, rocking her to dispel the wrenching disappointments.

Christmas was often worse. There were always mounds of presents, probably too many. I remember a lovely pale green dress that my mother gave her, and all Elene could come out with was sobbing and "I don't want any presents." There again was that lurking presence, that hidden threat in gifts, producing only tears.

Our response was simple. She was a highly sensitive and intelligent child, occasionally overwhelmed by emotional situations. That's all.

That was certainly the response of my mother, too. She felt she had a special relationship with Elene, who called her Mama Bet. I can remember summer days when we unfurled an inflated wading pool in the backyard among the orange trees. My mother would put on a bathing suit and get down into the one-foot water with Elene and they would splash and rollick and talk, talk, talk. My mother dreamt of Elene's teen years when she would take her on trips, show her Europe, and introduce her to the world.

But, sad to say, that was not to be. When Elene was eight, my mother succumbed to lung cancer. She was too young to die. We were all devastated, but no one as much as Elene.

One thing double-scored the tragedy—she died on Elene's birthday. There was no birthday party and obviously no presents. But that night Shirley woke me up and said she heard Elene crying. When I tiptoed into her room, she turned to me and her eyes were wide. She sat upright in bed. "Mama Bet came."

I said something like, "Yes. We all think of her tonight."

"No. I mean she came to me. Right here. The ceiling of my room split right open. Right there. And she walked through and talked to me. I talked to her, too."

My throat was dry. I said, "You already miss her."

"She told me she loved me and that she was sorry to have to go away."

"That was nice," I said. "I'll sit with you a bit." I tucked her in. "Try to go to sleep now."

Sitting on the edge of her bed in the dark, my thoughts churned. Do children of eight see visions and hear voices? Maybe it's common—there are always Neverlands and Narnias, but was this the same thing?

Elene still wet her bed, too. So because of that and because she had such trouble with presents and because she had now seen a vision, we took her to a psychiatrist, a young man, Dr. Will Franks, highly recommended by the school system. Elene's first visit with him was long. I waited in the car, and when he brought her, it was from around the corner where they had walked to Baskin-Robbins for an ice cream cone. That night Franks called us. He apparently had liked Elene very much. He had found her a normal but highly gifted child. In fact he said she was a model of how well adjusted an intellectual child could be. He dismissed the bed wetting as nothing to worry about. It would stop in due time of its own momentum. The fear of presents was a quirk that she would out-grow as well. Visions were not that unusual in children.

Franks was a liberated doctor. I thought of myself as liberated, too. The sixties were upon us and we were not immune. In those days college campuses had a way of radicalizing us. Franks felt that children, even young ones like Elene, should be exposed to all the exciting currents then abroad, especially those freeing individ-uals from the restraints of a doctrinaire past. He invited us to go with his family and some other parents and children to a showing of the musical *Hair* in Hollywood. *Hair* was being praised and damned as anti–Vietnam war, as an escape from authority, and above all, as an appreciation of the human body in all its nude glory. If a respected psychiatrist, Elene's own counselor, thought it a good idea, we didn't argue and joined a little caravan of cars with children of all ages trekking to the Earl Carroll Theater on Sunset Boulevard to see *Hair*. I can't believe Elene was "liberated" by the show, though who knows. She said nothing about the nude scene.

Elene clearly possessed a strong imagination. At least I'm assuming that music and imagination are somehow intertwined. She started music lessons by the time she was ten. Within a year I was envying her uncanny ability to sight-read music. She was able to open a never-seen sheet of Bach or Beethoven or Brahms and with a minimum of hesitation play the music. I listened in awe from the other room as she enlivened the old Knabe in our alcove. She never grumbled at music lessons.

Equally well she loved dance. In those years she studied dance with a couple of teachers in a downtown studio. Ballet became one of her delights.

In 1968, when Elene was twelve, I was awarded a Guggenheim Fellowship, the terms of which allowed me to study Western America as interpreted by British artists (especially those who had never been to America) in paintings, lithographs, and woodcuts. It was a faintly ridiculous subject for me since these were the years when my teenage uveitis was taking its toll, and my vision was growing dimmer and dimmer. I guess the choice of subject exposed a stubborn streak in me.

But whatever my study, the most intriguing prospect was the three of us living six months in London, and what those months would do for Elene—entering her teen years, seeing another part of the world, expanding her horizons, meeting new people, coming to know where Tennyson wrote of Elaine the fair, where Marlowe conceived of Helen's face launching a thousand ships. Neither Shirley nor I had ever been to England, and our excitement swept like wind in birches.

By phone and mail we leased a flat in Dolphin Square. The pictures showed a great rectangle of apartments around a rose garden along the Thames in Pimlico, just below Chelsea. We arrived on April 4, 1968, and found an England bathed in daffodils and just beginning to show tulips.

Of course, our expectations were far too high. The first sight of our flat was a letdown. It was on the ground floor and our windows looked out, not on the rose garden, but on a dark alley with a row of garbage cans. The furniture was dowdy: a heavily stuffed sofa, fringed lampshades, lace curtains, and firm mini-beds. The kitchen was barely big enough for one person, and what would be Elene's room was consumed by a small single bed, a wood chair, and a chest of three drawers. She barely had space to turn around.

I saw Elene's face drop and I felt mine dropping with hers. Shirley was upbeat. "The place is clean," she said, "and remember we'll only be here at night, so what difference does the view make?" We didn't say anything. She went on, "You unpack while I go out and get some staples."

I halfheartedly opened the suitcases and started in. I could hear Elene in her closet room. I went in and sat on her bed. She had to stretch over my knees when she passed with her clothes. She was folding everything tight and neat as she found proper places for each item in the drawers. She had brought a few books—*Winnie the Pooh*, *A Child's Garden of Verses*, *The Hobbit*, and the *Chronicles of Narnia*. She set them standing up on her dresser beside her comb and brush, also neatly placed.

When Shirley came back with coffee, cold cereal, milk, and bananas, I greeted her with, "We could look for another place."

"Why in the world would we do that?" Shirley laughed. "Besides, we signed a lease."

"We could break it."

"That's the last thing I want to do in England—fiddle around breaking leases." And she took the groceries with a frown into her little kitchen. Before long I could hear the teakettle whistling.

Though the flat was problematical, Shirley and I gloried in London. We took to it like burrowing prairie dogs, only popping up occasionally to catch our breath.

But with Elene it was not the same. Day after day she would choose to stay home in that cramped flat rather than go out and explore with us. At first we thought it was a passing phase, but weeks went by. When we insisted, she grumbled. We walked too slowly, she said. She wanted to walk fast and go more places.

So we thought she had reached the age of parental breach, embarrassed to be seen with her parents. We could excuse her on that score, but it still bothered us enormously. Here we were in London, a capital of culture and history, what should have been an exciting experience, and she stayed day after day in that dowdy Lilliputian flat, sleeping endlessly or reading.

We never stopped getting three tickets for great event Take, for example, a concert of Berlioz's *Te Deum* in St. Pa

Cathedral with Queen Elizabeth herself expected in attendance and our three seats on the main aisle where the Queen
would enter. Elene refused to go, and we ended with her empty
seat beside us. When the Queen and the prince with their ret-
inues appeared with fanfare, we could have reached out and
touched them. Oh, how it hurt to think of Elene sleeping and
moping at home.

One day we planned a day trip to Oxford. The night before as
Elene was going to bed, I said, "You'll enjoy seeing the haunts of
Lewis Carroll and C. S. Lewis tomorrow!"

She looked at me for a long time and then simply said,
"Good night."

Shirley and I were eating breakfast hoping for an early start.
Elene emerged in her robe, unwashed and uncombed.

"Better get ready," I said. "We want a full day there."

"I'm not going," she said.

I blew up. "Today you're going with us, no matter what you
want to do."

"You can't make me."

"Yes, I can. You get right in there and get dressed."

"I don't feel like going."

I began to shout. "I don't care. You're going."

She shouted back. "You walk too slow. I don't want to walk
with you."

"Then run circles around us. I don't care. You're going."

Shirley hated shouting matches. She said, "I'm all ready. I'll be
waiting down in the rose garden." And she picked up her coat and
umbrella and went out.

"What's the matter with Mom?"

"You know good and well. Now get in there and get dressed."
And I gave her a little push toward her room.

"I don't want to go with you." And she dodged behind a chair.

I tried to pull the chair aside and it flipped over. I tried to reach
for her and she started hitting me with her fists. She was crying
now. "I won't go. I won't go."

I kept trying to hold her, but she slipped away and ran out into
the hall.

I caught up with her and held her against the wall. "Why are you acting like this?"

She was screaming. "I'm not going!"

She was strong and jerked away from my hold. She ran into the apartment and into her room and slammed the door. In tears myself, I slowly retreated back. I picked up the chair. My stomach churned. I felt awful. Physical violence between us was new. I kept saying to myself, Why did I do that? Over a day trip to Oxford! How could anything be worth it?

I picked up my coat and hat. I went to her door and said, "We'll try to get back for a late supper."

It was one of those miserable days when you do what you're supposed to be doing but your mind is in a jumble. Shirley hadn't been in on the confrontation, so she was not that disturbed. "Don't worry," she kept saying all day, using different phrases. "She'll grow out of it." But among the spires of Oxford I kept thinking of Elene huddled asleep in her closet room.

Was the fault partially mine? That was not such a wild thought. My eyesight was continuing to dim, now noticeably. I couldn't see bus numbers. I got a pocket telescope so I could focus on them to catch the right bus. I found myself never crossing London traffic unless I walked with other pedestrians. My study subject took me to gallery after gallery, museum after museum, seeking versions of the American West and comparing them with Romantic paintings of other subjects such as North Africa or the Middle East. Increasingly I needed Shirley to describe details in the paintings.

What did all this mean to Elene? How does a child cope with a disabled father? Was "You walk too slowly" a cover for "Why aren't you whole like other fathers?" Shirley thought the idea was preposterous, but it bothered me.

There were nights when she seemed to say she was sorry. Shirley and I would come home for supper and Elene would have everything ready, the table set nicely with a few flowers, lamb chops from the shops on Lupus Street ready to broil. We loved those nights, trying not to think of her self-ordained confinement with a world of riches outside.

And I reasoned, too, as Shirley kept telling me, that maybe physical changes in Elene were behind the agoraphobia. That possibility was driven home one memorable night when Elene relented and went out with us. We had brought home tickets for the Covent Garden production of *Giselle*, and Elene's love of ballet momentarily overcame whatever resistance she harbored to going out with us.

The three of us sat amid the gold braid and red velvet of Covent Garden watching charming dancers and listening to captivating music. In the first intermission, Elene handed something over to Shirley. Shirley held up a tooth. Elene said, "It's my last baby tooth."

In the second intermission, I heard Elene whisper to Shirley, "Come with me." That night I learned from Shirley that Elene was having her first period. Life was dramatically announcing its transitions.

Nothing much changed in the remaining months. In hope we always bought three tickets, and usually turned the third back or sat beside an empty seat, our thoughts thrumming. What were we doing wrong? Is this what the teen years would be like? What mental quirks could account for her behavior?

Homeward bound, we crossed the Atlantic on the *S.S. France*. Another joy for Shirley and me; another agony for Elene. The dining room seemed to frighten her. She spent most of her time in the stateroom. By what could have been a wonderful coincidence, two slightly older kids of a Riverside colleague were on board, but they had no success in getting Elene into ping-pong games or ship activities. It consoled me a bit that it didn't seem to be just Shirley and me causing the agoraphobia, but that left the burning question—What was it?

Home again, and school, and resumption of a fairly normal life. It was Elene's last year in the gifted, ungraded program where she had been since the second grade. A team of the same teachers using the same room ushered twenty kids through six grades. I loved that program for Elene. I was so proud that she had been chosen—our gifted daughter, our blooming intellectual child.

A big shock came that fall. In the middle of the night Shirley and I heard faint sounds from the kitchen, too stealthy to be Elene. She seldom got up at night and if she did, she'd not be that quiet. We tiptoed down the hall to the kitchen. Peering around the door, Shirley said immediately, "It's Elene." But there was a throttled terror in her voice. "It's Elene, Robert!"

Elene was slumped in a chair fumbling in a drawer. Over her whole head was a thick plastic bag, the kind used to store food. The plastic was drawn in around her nose where her breath was caught. Her hair was all up inside the bag, as if she had allowed no obstacle to the intent. The enclosed hair made her face seem a distorted mask, a scrim of cobwebs. Around her neck was a cord—a heavy clothesline—pulled tight so that the plastic bag bushed out below it. Unaccountably I noticed the knot, a square knot, tied neatly, correctly, tightly.

A note and a ballpoint pen were on the table before her.

We flew in a panic, cutting the cord, ripping off the plastic. Elene's hair fell like dead leaves around her shoulders. I held her and watched her come back to reality. From far away I heard myself saying, "What happened? What got into you? What are you doing? What in God's name are you doing?"

Elene looked at me with wide, brimming eyes, still breathing fast. "If I had jumped off a bridge, I wouldn't have had a second chance."

Shirley picked up the note on the table. She tucked it in her robe as we got Elene back to her bed. I sat with her and held her hand. She cried a bit and then slowly drifted off to sleep as if she were exhausted. I sat there still stunned, watching her breathe, watching that lovely face settling into a peaceful rest. I didn't want to leave her, but Shirley came in, saw how well she was sleeping, and motioned me to come out.

Shirley's face was not as peaceful as Elene's. Tears had streaked her cheeks. Her hair was rumpled as if she had pulled her hands through it the wrong way. In our bedroom, she handed me the note and said, "Look at this."

The note said, "Good-bye, Mama and Papa. I want my eyes to be transplanted to Papa's." That was all.

My eyes blurred over. I read the note without meaning. I read it again, and it hit me like thunder. I was sinking into a lake of heavy mud, a quicksand of suffocation while questions blared. How long had Elene thought of giving me her eyes? Had she written the note long before? Had she sat and contemplated death, tasting the last bitter moments before the final decision? How could she imagine that I would let her eyes be transplanted to mine? Were there other reasons she wanted to take her own life? I almost hoped so, but I didn't want to hope so. She must be walking strange dream paths, strange mind paths. Had she strayed into some foreign fields beyond our reach? What makes a twelve-year-old want to commit suicide?

Shirley jolted me back to the moment. "I don't think she'll try it again. You heard her say if she had jumped off a bridge, she wouldn't have a second chance."

"I suppose. But what makes her want to die? Haven't we given her a decent life?"

"We'd better get her back to Dr. Franks. And I'll talk with Miss Wynns."

Shirley went reluctantly to bed. I returned to Elene's room, quietly to her side, and found her curled up, submerged in sleep, breathing deeply. Her cheeks were still ghostly pale and her forehead was furrowed. I wanted to touch it, to smooth it, to brush away tossing thoughts of dying, but I didn't dare wake her. If only I could enter her sleep world, what fairy tales of death might I find?

other. In short, the organization on an
t.

ay the lute, too?" I grumbled to Shirley.
I answered the door and there was
He was dressed in armor—dark green
it of mail made of interlocking rings
had constructed it ring by ring, piece
couldn't imagine how much time it
e gotten all those cans? And if they

mail. "It's pretty heavy," he said. I
could already smell his sweat. He
need some muscles to carry that

got a little of Michael's story. He
g top grades while he also played
me he had liked Elene from their
conference. He had found her
fun. And she knew tons of stuff,

. "And you're a senior."
He smiled.

ng, flowered dress and a veil
piece. I insisted on giving them
said hitching would be perfect-
bunting and hundreds of peo-
home worried as a hound dog.
. The organization looked like
king, smart, and energetic. At
boys. I couldn't help myself,
in San Diego.

up almost every weekend to
around our house, outside in
bbering away, often reading
or concerts in the park or on
ght her a small prayer rug,
es and turrets shadowed on

Chapter Four

Make Love Not War

Junior high school was not happy for Elene. She spent a lot of time in the principal's office with weak excuses for absence or tardiness. The saving grace came when the students from the gifted, ungraded program were allowed to take a few classes at the nearby high school. She took a modern dance class that intrigued her mightily. She also enrolled in an art class. She had always been talented in drawing. She brought home a male face drawn in charcoal from life—a callow young man with dark-circled eyes and a sad smile under bushy hair. It took my breath away; it was so good.

Later in the semester she brought home a four-by-six-foot canvas. The assignment was an architectural subject in oils using perspective. The large size was her choice. She spread out her paints and the canvas on the floor of our screened porch. Her composition was not unlike Matisse—the corner of a house with a garden visible through the windows. The end of the term came and the painting was due. To all intents and purposes the painting was finished. I offered Elene help in getting the canvas to school.

"Oh, no. It's not finished."

"It looks finished to me. I like it."

"I don't. I have to work on it."

"But isn't it due?"

"It's not finished."

Every day I watched her dab and dab at that painting. The last week of classes went by. She wouldn't turn it in. She wasn't satisfied. She got an incomplete in the course, and it drove me crazy. There was the painting, a perfectly good job, maybe even a particularly good job, showing a remarkable sense of perspective, vibrant colors, and contrasts. But she wouldn't turn it in. Whatever motivated her? Things had to be right, just right, and if they weren't absolutely right, there was no compromise. Was she so sensitive that she feared the least bit of criticism? She was like Michelangelo throwing her spatula at the Devil as she gazed into the face of God. Well, not quite. But that's the way I felt.

Music flooded our house. In between Brahms and Beethoven and Rachmaninoff Elene was introducing us to newer music. We all took to the Beatles. We loved Simon and Garfunkel, Peter, Paul, and Mary, Joan Baez, and Judy Collins. Musically we were right there with the sixties.

Elene got a summer job babysitting at a house only a bike ride away from ours. She reported for her new job Saturday morning. She lasted only one day. It seems she disagreed heartily with the strict discipline the parents imposed on the children and she even told the mother she shouldn't wad up the dishrag because that caused germs to multiply.

Shirley in disbelief cleared her throat. "You told them that?"

"They didn't clean the toilets right either."

I looked at Shirley, who was smiling at Elene. "Next time, dear, remember that parents have a right to raise their children as they choose, even wad their dishrags if they want."

About this time Michael Nickle entered our lives. Remember i was the late sixties and strange winds floated around colleges. Jil a history colleague of mine, asked Elene to go with her to a confe ence on J. R. R. Tolkien in a nearby college town. Since Elene h gobbled up *The Hobbit* and every volume of *The Lord of the Rir* we thought it a splendid invitation.

When they got back that night, they had a young boy them. He was introduced as Michael and it seems that Mic and Elene had spent much of the day together at the confer enjoying every scholarly paper on Gandalf and Frodo ar lyrics of *The Ring*. Jill had liked the boy well enough to brir

and sang ballads to one an
intellectual level checked o
"I suppose this kid can p
Early Saturday morning
Michael. I hardly knew him.
long johns covered with a su
from beer and soda cans. He
by piece. It looked fabulous.
had taken him. Where had h
had been beer, oh brother!

Inside he soon took off th
hefted, and it weighed a ton.
may be thin, but he would
around all day.

Elene wasn't ready yet so I
was a high school senior, gettin
drums in a rock band. He told
first meeting at the Claremont
lively, quick-witted, and lots of
he said.

"Elene is a sophomore," I said
"Our minds are the reverse."
Elene came beaming in a lo
wrapped around a cardboard head
a ride to the park, though Michael
ly easy. In the park were tents and
ple dressed and frolicking. I drove
I couldn't put my finger on my worr
fun. Michael seemed fine, good loo
fifteen, Elene was probably ready fo
though. I wished Michael had staye

But he certainly didn't. He came
see Elene. Sometimes they would sit
the garden under the orange trees, ja
poetry. Sometimes they would go off
the campus. One weekend he broug
maybe two feet by three feet with cast

wine red. It was clearly inexpensive when I felt it, somewhat strawish, but to Elene it was velvet. I heard them giggle as they nailed it to Elene's bedroom wall.

Shirley liked Michael. I was the hanger-back, and I kept telling myself I had no reason to be. We often let him sleep over. We had a little room with a bath in the back, separated from Elene's room by our bedroom. It seemed safe and decorous enough.

Six months later I found I was right to worry. Shirley picked me up at the office about five. She began quietly. "I have some news for you. You're not going to like this. Elene is pregnant."

Before it even seeped into my brain, I said, "It was Michael."

"Yes."

We sat there. The car was moving, but the world had stopped. I could have been in a hypnotic trance. I heard and saw nothing. Slowly I realized that Shirley was talking. "And she told me she knows when it happened. It was only once."

I came to consciousness enough to make a groan.

Shirley went on. "Remember that night he came up for the symphony on Saturday? He arrived Friday and we had dinner and talked 'til about ten. We tried to teach them bridge. When we went to bed, we left them in the living room. It seemed all right. They said they were tired and going to bed soon, too. That was our mistake. Not to get them off to their rooms before we went to bed."

"You mean it happened right in our living room?"

"Yes."

"I could throttle him. Don't let me near him!"

"He doesn't know and she doesn't want him to know."

"And why in God's name not?"

"Take it easy. She says she'll have an abortion."

"And Mr. Michael sits atop his sunny world tooting his harmonica."

"You let me handle this. I don't want you having a big row with Elene either, like you did in London."

"So all's right with the world. Amen!" My voice was cracki

"Nothing's all right. I know that. But your blustering isn't to make it any better."

Elene was quiet at dinner. She said something like "I know this is hard for you, Papa." And Shirley steered the conversation away. We talked about the Vietnam demonstrations Elene had joined that day, a march from the high school to the university. I could see her carrying a sign: Make Love Not War. And I shuddered inside.

The next day Shirley took Elene to Kaiser where a woman gynecologist confirmed the pregnancy. That doctor referred them to an obstetrician. They talked of options and concluded that an abortion, a D-and-C, would be the solution. But he was not allowed to perform the operation until Elene had been counseled by a special psychiatrist at the Kaiser facility in Hollywood. Shirley drove her in, and the psychiatrist talked with Elene alone for over an hour while Shirley sat in the dreary waiting room trying to read magazines whose words, I'm sure, ran together into gibberish.

I had come home early and was trying to play the piano, listlessly hoping to cover up all the thoughts fizzling in my mind. When the two came in the back door, Elene called back, "Don't worry, Papa. It's going to be fine." And she went to her room.

Shirley sat beside me. "It was an endless talk they had, but it seems OK. That doctor OK'd the D-and-C, even called the Kaiser obstetrician and made an appointment for next week."

"What did Elene say?"

"Very little. We were mostly quiet all the way home."

How many times have I tried to puzzle out Elene's feelings that week and the following. She seemed to be taking it matter-of-factly, assuming that at fifteen she couldn't take care of a baby and an abortion was the only way to go. She would not allow it to bother her too much. Those were the impressions I got when I talked with her, though she made it clear she didn't really want to talk about it.

I guess I wasn't that anxious to talk about it either. But I always knew that more was going on in her mind than she was letting on. There is nothing as lonely as a shut mouth; there is nothing as lonely as grief, and I was never sure that I didn't sense a fifteen-year-old's grief hidden in numbed recesses.

Years later I recalled that sense and wished I had acted on it. When she was in her thirties Elene was faced with another possibility of abortion. At that point she refused. This second time she unburdened herself to me, the words pouring out like the shadows of ancient buildings melting into thoughts. She told me how stricken she had been the first time, how babies are meant to be born. She put a cosmic twist on the fetus. She could not possibly intervene in that life's destiny. She would not have another abortion.

Michael never learned of the baby. Elene was already moving to the fringes of his attention. Weeks went by when he didn't appear. He had joined a troupe of street actors at the Sawdust Festival in Laguna and in San Diego's Old Town.

Elene was restless. Full-time high school held no lighthearted high jinks for her. Outside of the arts, she didn't like her classes. One year she was a National Merit Scholar, but she was collecting an impressive number of incompletes, usually in courses where projects like papers or stories or drawings were never turned in.

Increasingly at dinner she would eat and run.

"Is she all right?" I asked Shirley one evening after Elene had left and we were still finishing dessert.

"I think she's just busy—the beginning of her senior year, you know."

Not long after that, she announced at dinner that she wanted to go to the university and not finish high school.

"You need a high school diploma to enter the university," I said confidently.

"No, Papa, you don't."

"Look, I teach in the university, and I know you need a diploma to matriculate."

"If that word means enter, it's not true."

"OK, you go up to the university and talk with a dean. You'll learn otherwise. But if he says you can, I'll of course support the move." I felt safe enough.

"I think I'll do that, Papa."

She did. And she was right. She had sufficient grades in the subjects required for university entrance, and nowhere did it say that a diploma itself was required.

Having just turned sixteen, she would now enter the university in the spring term. And she would not have a high school diploma, now or ever. It was not my idea of the way things should go.

She started with two classes, four units each. Art History went fine. She loved to talk about paintings. She could go on and on about Monet's use of color, Matisse's sense of form, Mondrian's proportions. She got good grades there. But in Western Civilization she had to write frequent papers on the early Middle Ages and the Renaissance. The Society for Creative Anachronism didn't seem to help. Her papers had comments like "rambling," "unclear," and "unfocused." In that course Elene got a D.

A behavioral volcano was rumbling. She refused rides to the campus, always preferring to take her bike. Shirley made her nice clothes: jumpers, blouses, and smart pants, but she wore only white carpenter's overalls, everywhere, constantly. We would spot her all over town on her bike in her overalls, her long hair streaming. She was usually making the rounds of the health food stores, for she had become a vegetarian. Shirley and I respected her vegetarianism, and Shirley didn't mind cooking with that in mind. But Elene went further, using her allowance for ginseng tea, seaweed spice, and sunflower sprouts.

Rebellion brewed. She would wear nothing but those white carpenter's overalls, usually smudged with bicycle grease. She let her hair grow 'til it hung down her back to her waist. She spent most of her time away from home—on the campus, in parks, in libraries. In fact, she made it clear that she was not happy living at home, that she wanted an apartment of her own. It was hard to cope with her increasing grouchiness.

Shirley and I grew desperate.

"Is it a teenage thing?" I asked Shirley in the quiet of our bed. "When will it end?"

"Not soon. She's a stubborn young woman and she belongs to the sixties. We're part of the establishment, you know."

"She's not a young woman. She's a growing child."

"Oh? Tell that to her."

I tried. "You can't live alone," I said to Elene one night when she complained again about living at home. "You're not old enough."

"College students do, everywhere. Why can't you face the facts?"

"You're not a full-fledged college student yet. And beginning college students live in dorms."

She shrieked, "I'm a prisoner. And you're out of the dark ages. Don't you know times are changing?" She ran to her room, crying.

The first things to come flying out of her room were books. Her room was at the end of the hall, and now the door would open fast and something would be hurled out into the hall. Then came clothes, her good dresses, and sweaters that she hadn't worn for months, all in a heap. Jewelry followed. At first we tried to ignore her, assuming we would make her pick up when she calmed down. But there was fear in Shirley's eyes. In the living room we could hear glass breaking. I finally went to the hall. I saw an El Greco she had loved in London, its frame smashed. I picked up a folded drawing. It was a small pen and ink of a male face, head tilted back, laughing to the sky. I recognized Michael. I put the drawing in my pocket. I picked up the gold cross from Elene's baptism.

I called through the door. "Stop it, Elene! Stop it!" I went in. She was bent over drawers pulling things out. I tried to hold her. She was uncontrollable. Her strength was far greater than mine. "Get out of my room!" she screamed. I told her she would have to pick up every last thing, and stormed out.

"This can't go on," I said to Shirley later. "Let's get her an apartment. Let her learn that way."

We looked for apartments with Elene and agreed on one in a two-story sprawling complex in downtown Riverside. We knew it was crazy. We knew we shouldn't do it. But we also knew we couldn't cope with the situation at home. We thought the move wouldn't last.

The first night we left her there—what a welter of emotions. "Bolt the door carefully," I must have said three times. "Keep the phone close to your bed."

Her eyes held defiant fear. She was trying to be brave. What else could she do, I thought. She's frightened. What have we done?

Weeks went by. She biked home almost every day, ostensibly to get this or that. She wouldn't let us visit the apartment. We would offer to pick her up and take her to dinner or a movie. Absolutely not.

About the third week she began to sleep over at home. That always pleased us, but it obviously left her confused and irritable. Then one morning after she had stayed over, she wouldn't come out of her room. She holed up for days.

Shirley and I went down to her apartment. The door was unlocked. The place was outlandish, a mess of dirty dishes scattered everywhere, spoiled food, soiled clothes, open books, discarded papers. We went to the office, paid the rent, cleaned up the place, and closed out that phase of her development. I said to Shirley, "I guess we blew that one." But what I saw in the pile of trash was something terribly wrong, some crying hole in the tangled web of things, some missed opportunity. If there were some escape tunnel, where was it?

Chapter Five

A Desert Wind

Tense weeks followed in which Elene would not leave the house and stayed mostly in her room. When visitors came, she ran and hid. She refused baths. Her hair went unwashed for over a month.

I checked out books on agoraphobia from the library. Elene certainly fit the definitions—unreasonable intense fears in the presence of others, especially in public places, elevators, theaters, restaurants, and buses; manifested in a racing heart, sweating palms, churning stomach, tightening throat; often accompanied by extreme sensitivity to criticism. The articles claimed the condition was usually observed in early adulthood, often following a high-stress event.

These symptoms all applied in one way or another. I knew her palms had sweated. I had felt them. And I was reasonably sure her stomach was churning and her throat tightening, just to watch her. I knew if I held her hand, her pulse would be pounding and racing. Just the thought of it made my own stomach grab and groan. I so wanted to unwrinkle that pain she was feeling.

Agoraphobia was a mental illness and that term was beginning to creep into our minds. Like most of our friends, we had read Ken Kesey's early sixties book, *One Flew Over the Cuckoo's Nest*, and were chilled by prospects of Nurse Ratcheds and lobotomies. And in an early book of E. Fuller Torrey (*The Mind Game*) we were exposed to the idea that psychiatrists were no better than witch doctors. But we were a long way from putting Elene in any such context.

Most nights she ate with us, begrudgingly, and we made her help with the dishes, which she did reluctantly, claiming we were criticizing her lifestyle. One night she was washing and I was drying. She wore her overalls, but no blouse underneath.

"You've got to take a shower," I said. "You're beginning to smell pretty bad."

"I don't care. You're just uptight about natural things."

"It's not natural to be dirty. Look at your hair."

"It's fine. If I lived in an African village, that's the way it would be."

"You're not living in an African village."

"I wish I were."

She reached for something and raised her bare arm. Half-jokingly, I dashed some of the dishwater under her arm. "This'll help," I laughed.

She was furious. Her eyes sparked. We tangled. I tried to get more water on her. She tried to hold my hands. I wasn't that anxious to continue and she was strong, so we came to a halt, staring into one another's eyes.

"I don't understand you!" she cried. "I can never understand you. I can't see into your eyes. I can't see beyond that film, and I need to see into your eyes. How can I understand you if I can't see into your eyes?"

My muscles went limp. If there was a crying hole in the universe, Elene was looking for it, hoping to find the star gate to human understanding. And my cataracts were standing in her way. I stared into her eyes with my murky vision. I could see the black pupil, only partly dilated surrounded by the flecks of blue and green. She was looking back into my eyes, which I knew were completely dilated from daily drops, and I imagined the way they looked, the dilation exposing the milky capsule blocking entry. She began to cry. I could say nothing and she went sobbing to her room. Mechanically I finished the dishes. The next day she never emerged from her room.

Days went by, weeks went by, nearly two months went by and, except for occasional moments for a bite of food, Elene would not come out of her room, would not leave the house, would run off and cower if surprised by outsiders.

Often late at night, when the house was dark and silent, she came out and played the piano. Listening in our bed, I felt myself shaking at the haunting loveliness of her *Moonlight Sonata*, the wrenching chords and arpeggios of her Chopin nocturnes. I got up quietly, not disturbing Shirley, and took our back door into the yard where I could walk closer to the living room and listen without being seen.

It was late in the season and the highest oranges beyond reach were spoiling on the trees. Some had dropped and oozed a molding stench into the warm night. The music stirred that smell into a heady liquor. It seemed to distill her destiny. There was lacerating sorrow in the minor keys. I could feel sobs in the low notes. I imagined the solace she felt, her artist's soul soothed at the black Knabe reliving her childhood, music flooding her heart, draining her brain of demons. That old Knabe was only wood and wire and yellowing keys but she was converting it into a powerful force. How would I ever be able to fathom that force, to understand her? Is it love she seeks? Does she know how much I love her—how much Shirley loves her? Or is there some devil in her that denies and contradicts our love? Standing in my pajamas in the cool night, I shivered at the thought that something was drifting between us, like the heavy smell of decaying oranges.

I went back to bed but was still awake when the playing stopped. The silence was strange and lonely with only Elene's quick footsteps echoing in the hall toward her room.

Shirley and I grew desperate about the agoraphobia. What were we to do? We could not physically control her. She was no longer a child; she was a grown woman, young and strong. There was some fear in our reactions. Shirley had tried to force her to dress and come out, and in the tussle Elene had pulled wildly at Shirley's hair and once was ready to bite her when I pulled them apart. The pain, though, was in our desperation—the stifling, gagging feeling that we should be doing something but were blind to what it was. Finally we called the Riverside Community Mental

Health Department. Their crisis unit immediately sent two young women to the house.

Shirley and I poured out our story. They were a quiet pair, nice looking, and speaking like professionals. They talked of agoraphobia as serious but sometimes transient. And as we talked, it was easy to fall back into our assumption that Elene's behavior was that of an intellectually precocious, headstrong, rebellious late teenager who had drunk too deeply of sixties' philosophy.

The women asked if they could talk with Elene alone. Shirley took them to Elene's room. All we could hear for nearly an hour were muffled voices.

Leaving, the women said Elene had agreed to come down to their office next Tuesday morning. They assured us that all would be fine.

Tuesday came. Elene dashed into the kitchen for some breakfast. Her hair was still like matted glue and she was in her nightgown.

"What are you going to wear today?" Shirley asked.

"Why?"

"This is the day for the crisis unit. I'll drive you if you like."

"I'm not going."

My heart missed at least three beats.

Shirley said, "Didn't you agree to go?"

"I can't go today."

"I'll help you dress. You can bike if you'd rather."

"I can't go today. Don't you understand?" And she ran off to her room.

I took a deep breath. "We're getting nowhere."

I called the crisis unit, and they said they understood completely.

Elene had a portable radio in her room and she listened frequently to KPFK, a station that broadcasted classical music and concentrated on the arts in general. One day she emerged from her room and said defiantly, "Have you ever heard of Isomata? It's on the radio. I think I would like to go there."

I did know about Isomata. It was a school for the arts run by USC in the pines of Idyllwild. "It's a good place," I said. "What would you study?"

"Dance, of course. They do both modern and ballet."

It was not dance that registered on my mind but the prospect of getting Elene out into the world again, out of that room, away from her fears of other human beings. Isomata might be our salvation. Bless Isomata. Where do we register?

She was accepted for the summer session. We paid the fees. The day we were to go she was ready, dressed, her hair covered with a bandanna, and carrying her bag with clothes for two weeks. Her eyes darted fearfully as she sat in the backseat. Shirley drove, as always now because of my vision. I sat in the front passenger seat.

On the mountain road we said little. It was a fragile situation. I feared the wrong word might break the spell. When we got to Isomata, she bravely marched into the dormitory where she had been assigned a suite with eight other women. We got her settled, saw her introduced to the only other girl who had yet arrived, and then we took off, not wanting to linger and prolong the possibility of backing out.

We called her almost every night during those two weeks. She didn't want us to come up for a visit. We talked with a counselor who said Elene was working terribly hard, spending most of her time in the practice rooms. The counselor seemed proud of her, not worried. Grasp at straws, ye parents, and live in hope.

Two weeks later we drove to Isomata to bring Elene home. Shirley and Elene walked down to the administration office to turn in keys and check out. I stayed back in the dorm room, putting the last things together. When finished, I waited in the sitting room. There were two other girls also waiting there. I asked if they knew Elene.

"No one knew Elene," answered a dark-haired woman in her early twenties. "She was always working."

The other girl chimed in. "I don't think Elene even knew my name and we both lived in this same dinky suite. I saw her at meals but she didn't eat much, only vegetables. Didn't eat many of those, even."

"She's had a few problems lately," I said meekly.

"I'm not surprised," the older one said. "I found her once in the closet, just sitting there, I guess to avoid talking with us. I don't think we were that bad."

The first girl added, "She kept bringing back leftover bits of food from the dining room. Our fridge began to stink with all her wrapped dabs of broccoli and fish."

My brain became an ants' nest, stirred by a stick into a squirming mass. So it hadn't worked. Our hopes had been false. I walked out to the car. I thought I smelled broccoli instead of the pines. When Shirley and Elene returned, I noticed that Elene's hair was as gluey as ever. She looked terribly thin. Her eyes dominated, round and staring.

"All ready?" I said.

"I have things in the refrigerator."

"Let's toss them out and start fresh at home."

"No. I want to take them."

"They'll be spoiled by now," Shirley said.

"I know when things are spoiled."

She was collecting armloads of foil-wrapped bits and pieces from the refrigerator. They filled all the extra places in the back of our trunk. We knew they would have to be thrown out eventually.

Elene talked a lot on the way home. She seemed to have liked the experience. She said she loved walking to dance class in the early morning, passing dorms from which came practice strains of piano or clarinet or cello.

I pictured her in the closet, and hoped against hope that it was only once.

At home Shirley noticed that Elene's ankles and feet were badly swollen.

"How long has that been?"

"Just the last day or two."

"I think we'd better let Kaiser check you out."

Elene was frightened enough by the ankles to agree. The doctor thought she was lacking in protein, not eating properly. "Take her home. Feed her up. I think I can trust you to do that."

Elene was smart enough to be scared, so she cooperated. Shirley cooked wonderfully the next month—lots of protein-heavy lentils and grilled tofu and eggplant hummus. Elene slowly regained energy. Her face filled out. It was like watching a peach ripen and take on color.

But like a maelstrom, her room pulled her back into its orbit. She couldn't go out. She ran to her room or hid when visitors came. Isomata had not changed the picture.

Without telling Elene, Shirley went down to the Crisis Center and talked with the women who had interviewed Elene three months earlier. They listened to the whole story and came up with a chilling conclusion. "You may have to hospitalize her, you know."

Shirley told me they recommended the psychiatric ward at Loma Linda.

"It's horrible. I don't want to even think about it."

My sleep was weighted with memories of Olivia de Havilland's descent into the "snake pit" in the old movie and the terrors of Ken Kesey's Nurse Ratched in *One Flew Over the Cuckoo's Nest*. I woke often that night. I couldn't put her in such a setting. She was an attractive young woman, basically strong with a well-developed body that might well pull her through this crisis. She had a mind full of ideas and an artistic talent that was able to express her thoughts beautifully. I didn't want to remember her as she looked at Isomata. I knew her as pretty with bright hazel eyes and soft brown hair worn long. Her prominent nose always gave her an aristocratic touch. I couldn't see her in the snake pit. I couldn't make her a candidate for a psychiatric hospital.

In fact, she herself came up with an alternative. In *Prevention*, a health magazine of Shirley's, Elene had seen an ad for the Vita Dell Spa in Desert Hot Springs—special vegetarian diets, natural hot springs, expert exercise counselors trained in yoga, and one instructor even offering modern dance.

Shirley sent for the brochures. Pictured were the participants' rooms ranged around the pool and spa like a motel. Dining, gym, and recreation were at the other end. One picture showed a piano in the recreation room. That was a good sign. The tuition was $700 a week, but that was nothing compared with a hospital. And more important, Elene wanted to do it. Even though Isomata hadn't worked, maybe this emphasis on health, instead of an emphasis on art, would.

The three of us made the hour and a half drive through the San Gorgonio Pass and out onto the desert to look over Vita Dell. We found it on the edge of settlement among creosote bushes and salt weed. A young woman, tan and muscular, gave us a tour. It didn't appeal to me—too much concrete, too many closed doors, too many infernal machines in the gym, one of which turned you upside down.

I considered Vita Dell too spartan, the sparkling blue pool being the only spot that appealed to me. But Elene was pleased. We talked with the woman in charge, Dr. Lydia Oneonta, a chiro-practic doctor in a loose white coat. Her voice was crisp, suggest-ing capability and attention to immediate business. My misgivings all seemed silly, and I didn't even voice them. The important thing was that Elene liked the place and wanted to stay for a time, maybe a couple of weeks. For Shirley and me the prospect of getting her out of her rut and into the world of people again was overriding.

So in May we drove her out with her suitcases and shopping bags of indispensable herbs. That day was probably one hun-dred degrees.

Her room was sterile and uninviting. But our minds dwelt on the plusses—she would at least be with people.

Elene continued upbeat. In our phone conversations we regularly suggested coming home. "Oh, no," she said. And she told us of dawn hikes with the young people, of cool evenings sitting in the hot mineral springs. Shirley and I ate up those positive reactions. We, after all, were living in an aura of des-perate hope.

June 24, 1972, was our twenty-third wedding anniversary. We went out for dinner. Elene had been at Vita Dell for almost a month. When we got back the answering machine had a call from Desert Hot Springs.

We returned the call. "We've been trying to get you for hours," Dr. Oneonta scolded. "Elene is out of hand. We can't control her. You must come and get her immediately."

We were on the road by eight thirty. It was a hot night, even for summer in the desert. The wind was howling. It swerved us along like a soccer player hurrying a ball toward the goal. When we knocked and opened Elene's door, she began immediately to rant at us. "The auras are everywhere. Can't you see them? Yours are dark. Your aura is full of poisons. You've got to clear your aura. It's telling you that. They're poisoning me here. Don't let them poison me. Can you see my aura?"

The room could have been hit by a tornado. Clothes were crumpled together with papers. Plastic cups were squashed between half-filled cups of juice. The bed was stripped to the mattress and all its bedding was in a heap in the corner. The bathroom had open jars and squeezed tubes everywhere. Something was soaking in the sink. The toilet was unflushed. I flushed it without thinking.

"You're wasting water," she yelled. "The spiders drink from there. They need to live, too. You never think of the spiders."

"Let's get your things together," Shirley said to her softly.

"Your auras are wrong." She was looking hard at Shirley. "They come in and spray for the spiders. It's terrible. They're poisoning me."

I found some boxes in her closet and began throwing things in them and hauling them out to the car, the wind banging doors like an angry belligerent.

I kept saying to her, "You'll be fine, Elene. Help us pack. We'll be home in no time."

She roamed around the little room, talking constantly over the wail of the wind. Whenever we threw something in the trash basket, she would pull it out. "I need this." Her voice was loud and sometimes fretfully incoherent. She was holding paper cups in each hand.

"You don't care anything about the ecology, do you? That's why your aura is so black. Auras are..."

At one point Shirley and I were both at the car, fighting the wind, trying to rearrange the boxes and bags and cases in the trunk. When I got back to the room, Elene was in the bathroom. The door was half-closed.

At first I thought she might be on the toilet, so I didn't look, but then I noticed through the crack that she was standing before the mirror. Even with my fuzzy vision I could tell she was wielding a huge pair of scissors and cutting off her hair in big swatches. The floor was already littered with the piles. Her hair had been long, cascading down her back or braided over her head. Now it was coming off close to the scalp in jagged clumps. I rushed in.

"Elene! Don't do that. What are you doing?" I tried to stop her, to hold her hands. But she was strong. She had a firm grip on the scissors. I couldn't see well enough to know how to do it, and the scissors scared me, too. She was in no state to be clutching anything sharp, and the scissors must have been a foot long.

She never stopped talking. "This will help my aura. The spiders will help me." Suddenly she threw down the scissors and put her finger to the back of the sink. She let a daddy longlegs crawl along her finger and the back of her hand. "He wants to help." Behind her back, I quickly retrieved the scissors and threw them in the bottom of a bag with other things on top. Then I looked at her spider and said, "Let's take him with us."

"We won't hurt him, will we?"

"Of course not." I called to Shirley. "Elene and I are getting in the car. Will you finish up?" I knew she would understand the importance of making that transition to the car, and there wasn't too much left to jam in the trunk.

So Elene and I climbed into the backseat, Elene carefully keeping the spider on one hand or the other and studying it closely as she absently got in with me. I locked the back doors with us inside. She rambled on about the auras of spiders. I professed great interest and kept her talking. My heart was breaking as I looked at her hair, jagged, scalp exposed in places, a matted pad in others. I couldn't see her eyes, but I knew they must be wild.

Shirley had gone over to the office where Dr. Oneonta, between expressions of sympathy and denials of accountability, had her sign releases. When she returned, we both knew that I must remain in the backseat with Elene, talking, soothing, restraining. Otherwise Shirley would have been too frantic to drive.

It was after midnight. Off we went onto that windy highway, trucks swaying, tumbleweeds scooting, sand blasting. The wind was stronger than before and we were now headed right into it, no longer a friendly assist but a bitter enemy beating against our advance. The wolf-howl of the wind seemed to calm Elene. Her jabber came slower and slower. Her head drooped on my shoulder and I held her hand. I don't know what happened to the spider.

A strange, soothing stillness fell inside, against the moan of the manic wind and the whirr of tires struggling to go faster than the wind permitted. Shirley's head was a blur for me against the headlights in the night.

Within that stillness, my mind was as wild as the wind. I wanted to talk with Shirley but I didn't dare speak and break the spell. Where were we headed? Home, of course, but what would happen there? It would then be about two in the morning. Maybe Shirley could heat up some soup. Maybe Elene would remain calm and sleep the rest of the night and we could assess the situation in the morning. Another part of me said, Dreamer. She's pretty far gone. She'll need more than a bowl of soup.

But then I would argue back. Maybe Elene had a point. Maybe Vita Dell *was* poisoning her, at least in the sense that their regimes were doing her harm. And who knows whether we have auras or not? There are electrical fields around us, aren't there? Or something like that. And spiders might very well need protection against spraying. If I loved spiders more, as she does, I'd not want to see them sprayed to death. Oh, but Robert, she wasn't saying those things as rationally as you are. They were coming out like jumbles, yes, like crazy.

When we pulled into our garage, Elene woke up and began to jabber again, almost as if she had been wound up. "Don't let them kill me. The bombs will come, you know. But I can stop them, if they'll let me."

In the house, she wouldn't sit down. Shirley heated some vegetable soup, but Elene wouldn't have any. Shirley and I had some, and got ready for bed, hoping Elene would calm down. When we came out in our pajamas, she had taken off her clothes and was roaming around naked. "I can be Jesus when I want to be," she was saying. "I can be a savior. I have special powers." She was talking loudly now, almost screaming. She was in the kitchen. "You don't need all these things." She took up a ceramic salad bowl and crashed it to the floor. "There're too many things here. I want to go back to Vita Dell." A water pitcher came down in pieces, fortunately big pieces that she managed to avoid with her bare feet. "I'm a savior, you know."

In our bedroom Shirley said, "We can't let this go on. I'm scared."

"Can't we make it through the night? There's not much left of it."

"No. I'd be scared to spend the night this way."

"You mean the emergency room?"

She nodded.

"Loma Linda?"

She nodded again, and we pulled on some clothes.

Elene had broken a few more dishes and had pushed over a houseplant in the living room. I went to her. "Elene, did you say you'd like to go back to Vita Dell?" I thought that might get her into the car.

She did not answer but only said, "There are too many things here."

Shirley came with a warm robe and we slowly edged her back to the garage and into the car. We headed up the freeway through Redlands toward Loma Linda. I was holding Elene's left hand. She was jabbering about the bombs in the world.

We were only a few miles on the way when I looked with horror at what she was doing. She had quickly held her arm to her mouth and had bitten a sizable piece out of her forearm. The blood was already flowing.

"Elene," I screamed. "What are you doing?"

"Don't worry, Papa. It's nothing."

The blood was running everywhere. I pulled out a handkerchief and wrapped it around the wound. And I tied a cotton sweater tight around that.

"Don't stop," I said to Shirley. "Just get us there."

As I held the wrappings tight, Elene began to cry.

"We'll get you to a doctor, sweetheart," I said.

"No. No," she sobbed.

I looked above her head to the east where the clouds were streaked with dawn.

Shirley went into the emergency room. Before long, attendants came out with a gurney and we got her on it, ranting sadly, pitifully. In the neon of the parking lot she was unrecognizable with her hair whacked off and her eyes swollen with tears. I watched the attendants roll her away. In a daze Shirley and I followed, holding onto one another, not too certain of our steps. When we got beside her again in the emergency room, the nurses were already cleaning and bandaging her bitten arm. When the doctor came in, she was screaming, "No! No! I don't want to be here!" The doctor did a cursory examination of her eyes, listened to her heart, and asked us to step outside.

"We cannot keep her," he said.

"What do you mean, you can't keep her?"

"She has to be stabilized, and we can't do that. We're not equipped to."

"So what happens?"

"We'll send her to the county hospital for stabilization. Then if you want her here, they will send her back. It shouldn't be more than a day or two."

"Should we go with her?"

The doctor must have taken one look and put us down as potential patients ourselves. He said, "No. The ambulance will be best. At the moment you will not be needed."

A nurse had us sign a sheaf of papers—consent for treatment, insurance plans, something called a seventy-two-hour hold, and finally she explained that Elene would be eligible for SSI, the federal support system for the disabled. She gave us the forms and said we should apply as soon as possible.

Groggy may not be strong enough to describe our feelings. Shirley drove us home. She must have been more tired than I was. The dawning sun broke through the June mist but only slowly registered on us.

At home we swept a path through broken glass in the kitchen, ate an orange, and fell into our bed. When I awoke around noon, Shirley was not beside me. I took a while to recognize the sound of the broom brushing the kitchen floor of glass and pottery. I wondered what she was thinking as she assessed the breakage. I hated to get up. I hated the world. I hated to face the day.

Eventually I called the Mental Health Unit of the Riverside County Hospital. Yes, Elene was there, the nurse said, and was responding nicely. We could see her anytime.

We took hot showers to placate the remaining fatigue. Bless hot water.

Riverside County Hospital was a pile of concrete a full block long, a huge institution. At the mental health unit, an attendant took down our names, address, and phone, then disappeared. He returned and with a great ring of keys opened the first door. We stood in the decompression chamber while the first thick door swung locked, then he unlocked the second door. The process reeked of criminals. Shirley and I were very quiet.

We were ushered down a hall into a big social room. There were men talking to themselves or laughing with one another. A television blared with no one watching. There were women staring; there were Chicanos and Blacks and Asians; there were baggy, T-shirted Anglos.

A nurse brought Elene in. The pupils in her eyes were large and restless. I rose and started to hug her.

"Don't hug me," she said loudly. I dropped my arms and reached for her hand.

"Don't touch me."

My frustration was overpowering. I wanted so much to hug her. She looked so pitiful. She needed comforting, protection from all those blue devils. She needed hugging. But I didn't want to upset her, and she was adamant. She repeated, "Don't touch me."

Was I repulsive to her? Did she feel herself somehow untouchable? Did she imagine that the medications would contaminate us? The blue devils could reach out and grab us, too. It was a crazy thought, but I wasn't thinking too clearly either.

Shirley had brought the SSI forms, and she used them now to insert a leaven in the situation.

"Elene, I've brought along some forms. It's called SSI, and it's a kind of way to help us pay for the hospitals. You must sign them. I've filled out all the blanks except your signature." Elene seemed unconcerned about the meaning. She took the pen from Shirley and started to write where Shirley was pointing. Her hand went high and her mark started in the printing.

"Can I do it?" She looked sadly at Shirley.

"Let's practice a bit." Shirley offered some scratch paper. Elene tried and tried. The marks went wildly around like unresolved doodles, but gradually centered and conformed until she took the forms and wrote her name, large and awkward but readable. She looked up proudly, her gaunt eyes shining a bit. "I did it? Didn't I?"

My throat was tight. I kept trying to swallow, but it was hard. I went over to a machine and brought back two cans of Hansen's apple juice. I knew Elene would drink that, but not things like Coke or Sprite. I brought her a cup. She drank a little.

Elene was three days in the Riverside Hospital before they called her stabilized. I talked with the psychiatrist. He would make no diagnosis.

I didn't believe him. How could he decide on medication without making some kind of diagnosis? Were there automatic medications for every emergency mental patient? I couldn't believe that. In any case, the doctor wasn't revealing his secrets to me.

"She'll be fine," he kept saying. "Loma Linda's a good place. We're too crowded here."

At Loma Linda the double locked doors seemed less purgatorial. I wondered if it was the carpet. Shirley thought it was because it was smaller, on one floor in a round building so that the patients' rooms radiated out like spokes from the central nursing station. There were four patients to a room, but still I felt something personal about the atmosphere. We were sitting in one of the spokes that had upholstered chairs, not plastic. The adjoining spoke was a kitchen. Patients were opening the fridge and taking out drinks.

We saw the nurse bringing Elene, and my heart sank. She seemed little better. She walked like a zombie, shuffling, hesitating. She stared straight ahead and as she got closer I noticed her eyes weren't focusing on anything.

She sat down beside us and the nurse left. "I can't stay here," she said in a monotone.

"It seems like a nice place," I ventured.

"They make me take these horrible pills. I have cramps. I can't read. Everything is blurry."

I noticed she was trembling. Shirley said, "Can I hug you?"

"No. You don't want to."

"I do. Very much."

"I can't stay here."

"Maybe it won't be long," I said.

She made a sigh like wind through tall grass. She put her hand to her head and I could see her arm, still bandaged, shaking. "I can't stay here," she said, and as if she meant she couldn't stay in that chair, she rose unsteadily and shuffled away to her room.

Shirley and I sat and watched her go, like two people who had seen a ghost. I closed my eyes, hoping to blot out what I had seen, but the image of Elene—uncontrolled, shuffling, shaking—filled my mind's eye as well. Neither Shirley nor I spoke as the nurse smiled at us knowingly and let us out the double locked doors.

I talked with the psychiatrist that same day. "She's doing fine," he said.

"It didn't look that way to me," I grumbled.

"She's on Haldol. It's a powerful drug that reorders the dopamine in the brain. You're seeing the side effects, which can be unpleasant, but I'm working on them with other medications."

I said nothing for a moment and then went on softly, "I hope you can keep her from cramping and shaking and not being able to read."

"I think we can do that. I can increase the dosage of the Navane."

I felt terrible, as if he was leading us into a swamp and only he knew the directions. But the swamp was a tangle of sorrow. What had happened to Elene? What had happened to that talented mind that could make drawings that brought tears and play music that charmed? Now that same mind led her to whack off her hair, bite pieces of her own arm, shake, blur, and shuffle. And I stood by helpless, not even able to hug her or quiet the shaking with love. And there was always the possibility that it was our fault—that Shirley and I had done something wrong, had raised her wrong, not been firm, been too firm at the wrong times, not expressed our love enough—there were so many possibilities. And they all muddied the waters of that poisonous swamp. I thought of the night with the plastic bag. On that night she had not given me her eyes, but she had lost her own vision. Now she could not read. Now we shuffled with the spirit of that sweet young girl through the mud of this murky swamp.

Chapter Six

Smoke Alarms

Elene had been home from Loma Linda for several weeks. She continued to take Haldol but a much lower dose. Her mind seemed clear, though she still trembled and cramped. She said she could live with that for a while.

Now we were preparing for, of all things, an extensive trip. We were on our way to Santa Cruz, and the trip had been a hard decision—to take Elene away from home so soon after the hospital. It was instigated by a sabbatical I had that fall. With Elene's situation in mind, it was troubling to imagine how we might take advantage of the leave, but we eventually came up with a scheme that in retrospect seems crazy but at the time made sense.

In the first place, I had abandoned Western art as a subject, bowing to my waxing blindness. As a substitute I returned to communal experiments, where I had begun my scholarly life. Since our times, the sixties and seventies, were rife with such communities, and since I could visit and study and interview these new groups without a great deal of manuscript reading, seeing through Shirley's eyes when necessary, I changed to the study of modern communes. Northern California was a seedbed for such groups, and Santa Cruz and the mountains behind it were alive with them. That was one consideration.

Santa Cruz also housed a young campus of the University of California. The campus was experimental and appealing—divided into small live-in, personalized colleges, many of which were closely attuned to the counterculture of the sixties. Wouldn't that be an environment where Elene could feel at home and maybe thrive?

Most important, Shirley and I reasoned that a change of scenery might be good for the three of us, especially Elene. Riverside had collected memories like leeches on our backs—the suicide attempt, the abortion, the months holed in a bedroom, the failed apartment, the Isomata anorexia, Vita Dell and the windy nightmare, two hospitals and the horrors of Haldol. All three of us could stand a change. If we went together, there would be no trauma of parting, and Elene might find her way back to the real world more easily than if she were closer to the memories.

To clinch our thinking I was offered a visiting professorship at one of the new UCSC colleges, Kresge, including visiting-faculty housing. Elene could transfer her student status from the Riverside campus. We checked with her doctor at Loma Linda, and he thought the change could do no harm.

We loaded our Ford station wagon and closed up the house. Elene climbed into the backseat, not overjoyed but resigned. Her hair was combed cleverly and covered with a scarf. I watched her get in and swallowed hard. I saw under her bandanna both a fragile gypsy and a taciturn young woman, fearfully disguising her past. And we were putting her in a gypsy wagon to rumble six hundred miles. How balmy can you get!

But we were then reasonably optimistic, loaded with suitcases, bags, and boxes, driving off that early morning in late August 1973 for the seven- or eight-hour trip. Late that same afternoon we ascended the long hill that leads to the UC campus in Santa Cruz. We stared at its beauty—the redwoods framing meadows that sloped above the silver Pacific. The air smelled of grasses and needles and sea. A student restaurant at the college, all wood and glass and plants, was across the enclosure, filled with chatting young men and women. Shirley and I were enchanted.

The apartment was small, very small: a sitting room that included a hot-plate kitchen and one bedroom with twin beds and a rollaway. It was on the second floor, with no elevator, and though

I could manage the stairs, the prospect of tumbling down them gave me some pause.

We sat on the beds amid our piles of stuff.

I said it first. "Three months in this tiny space and the three of us will be at each other's throats."

"I fear you're right."

I proposed that Elene stay in this apartment and we look for a place nearby, without stairs. We found a studio apartment in a homey motel with a blossoming garden. We reasoned that Elene, free of us, would sit with fellow students in that plant-filled restaurant, walk with friends to class through scented woods, and gradually disperse the agoraphobic shadows in her brain.

But new shadows edged out the old. They became more than shadows, more like boiling fears. She feared the sprinkler system in the ceiling of her room, and she believed the smoke alarm was poisoning her with unseen rays and toxic fumes. It turned out that our nearness was not so much a consolation as a trap. We had rented her a bicycle, and it was easy for her to cycle down to our place. Before long she was spending most of her time with us, eating meals, sleeping overnight on the floor. She said she felt shaky every time she went out on the campus.

But she wasn't happy with us either. Nothing we did seemed right. Our food was all wrong, our clothes were too traditional, and our ideas were Neolithic. She was gradually taking over our motel room with her clothes and coffee cups. She had registered and was attending classes, so books and papers cluttered the place.

Every day Shirley and I visited communes in the hills behind Santa Cruz. But our doings didn't please Elene. She called our surveys "invasive," "intruding on people's privacy."

"They seem to like our coming," I said. "We always take a big bag of oranges or apples."

"And you think that's enough? Buying them off so they'll say nice things? They're laughing at you."

She was inadvertently raising legitimate questions about historical informants—the way situations color information.

I lamented her fears, but I wasn't about to discount her reasoning powers.

She came to us one night and said she wanted to go to the hospital. She was shaking. She said her eyes wouldn't focus. The smoke alarms in her apartment were fuming her to death. She couldn't go back there.

She slept with us that night and the next day we made an appointment with a psychiatrist, Dr. Leon Most, who arranged for Elene's admission to the Dominican Hospital mental health unit. With drooping hearts, we took her down.

The facility surprised us. We were confused at first; it seemed so unlike a hospital. It was new, a low, rambling building separate from the multistory hospital. The structure was all wood, redwood board-and-bat, not unlike our house in Riverside. Social workers, wearing jeans and bright shirts, took her into the women's wing, and we noticed that the locked door was single and wooden, not metal and double as in previous hospitals. Elene stayed there five days.

We met Dr. Most. Elene liked him. We liked him. When we all three sat with him, Shirley noticed that he winked at Elene as if they had a secret between them.

When I talked with him alone, I outlined Elene's previous history. But he refused to make a diagnosis. In cases like this, he said, we simply can't differentiate between the affective disorders and the potentially psychotic states. He felt that all of Elene's problems might possibly be solved by time and a little rest.

I wanted a clear diagnosis and prognosis but we weren't getting it. I kept thinking of Torrey's description of psychiatrists as witch doctors, but they didn't seem like witch doctors as much as procrastinators. Meanwhile we were optimistically driving blind.

The five days in the hospital did seem to get Elene back into shape. She still stayed with us a lot, but she wasn't as terrified of her apartment as she had been.

September, October, and November went by without serious incident. By then we had talked ourselves into believing that the time had come for Elene to try it alone, that our leaving would allow her to buckle down and get on with her life.

For the coming winter term Elene got a student three-bedroom suite including kitchen that she would share with two other girls. It seemed an ideal situation. In mid-December, my sabbatical and Elene's term over, we helped her get her new room organized, clothes in drawers and closet, bed made, a few staples in her designated kitchen cupboard. Then the three of us drove back to Riverside to enjoy Christmas before Elene returned to her new life.

I don't remember much from the holidays that year. I seem to recall a lot of arguments between Shirley and Elene. I suspect they were both tense over the coming separation. I'm sure we didn't exchange presents with Elene. I had come to accept her attitude toward presents as a part of her strength, her stand against an acquisitive and grasping world. Surely there was nothing wrong with that.

The day after New Year's we took Elene to the Greyhound bus for the trip back to Santa Cruz. She carried in one hand a clutch of dried flowers and in the other her favorite teapot, brown with painted daisies, wrapped in thin tissue paper.

We helped her up the steps of the bus. Her eyes darted and I saw fear in them. It was hard for her to wave with her arms full, but she smiled weakly from the window. Only a few months from the Santa Cruz hospital, still terrified of smoke alarms, our daughter was leaving us.

"Oh, Shirley," I moaned on the way home. "What have we done?"

"Maybe given her independence. That's not a little thing."

"Is she ready for that? Or just headed for more trouble?"

"I think it's right for now. We irritate her."

"She still seems so fragile."

"Right now she strikes me as the pluckiest person I know."

We called her about nine. She was in her room, had met the other women, and, miracle of miracles, the teapot had made it, too. We slept soundly that night.

All winter and spring we talked often with Elene on the phone and drove up a couple of times. From what we could tell, things were fine.

In June she told us that she would use her dorm rent for a room with other students in a big house on Rigg Street. She had been bitten by the prevailing student craze to live off campus.

"Don't like the sound of that," I said to Shirley.

"You can talk to her if you want, but I'm not going to. She's a determined young woman, and I for one am not prepared to cut off her funds."

On our next trip that summer we saw her room. It was another small one, about the size of her space in London. But what could we say? She seemed happy and was saving money.

We took Elene to Nature's Harvest for dinner. The menu was strange, with terms I only vaguely knew—chai, ginseng, vegan, microbiotic, wheatgrass, alfalfa sprouts. Elene suggested we try tofu scrambled with vegetables. We drank a fruit smoothie and then chai tea. It was good. I wouldn't have any trouble adding tofu and chai to our diet. Elene had expanded our lives.

Later Shirley and I debated that point, too. I wondered, "Maybe we shouldn't accept her ways so easily. A small matter, tofu, but maybe parents should say 'ridiculous' and order a slice of roast beef. That way roles don't get blurred."

Shirley laughed. "Honestly, you can worry about the silliest things. If you like tofu, eat it. Believe me, it doesn't say anything about you as a parent. It's like that old joke that real men don't eat quiche. Do you think real fathers don't eat tofu?"

Walking down the streets we were surprised at how many long-haired, bearded, Hindu-shirted men Elene knew—Baba and Dass Krishna and Shooting Star.

She told us they had all dropped out of the university, having realized its dangers.

"I've never thought it dangerous."

"It's blocking change. It's holding up a society that's dying."

"I didn't know that."

We started getting six- and seven-page letters from her. The writing was in letters half an inch high. I never knew whether that was her present writing style or whether she was doing it for my vision. Her intellectual life was expanding like a helium balloon. She wrote of Nabokov and Anaïs Nin and Ram Dass. She wrote about Christina Stead, her favorite author that week. "She resolves less about the human condition, but her characterizations and situations are amazingly vivid. I think you would love her writing."

Elene's painting class made field trips to San Francisco. One was to see a show of Jean Arp. She wrote, "My favorites were the dull bronzes, though the shiny bronzes had more linear edges and generally seemed sharper and crisper, brighter in their energy. They seemed more alive than some of Moore's figures and they ask to be caressed or nestled up into." I ate those letters like manna. They said to me that she was not only growing intellectually, she was functioning at a high level. I loved the thought of my daughter enjoying Jean Arp and Henry Moore and, even more, critically and artistically comparing them.

Shirley said, "Dr. Most must have been right—nothing wrong with her that time can't cure. I think he thought of her as a teenager whose mind was ready for the call of the counterculture."

Next fall Elene obeyed another counterculture dictum—"Tune in, turn on, and drop out" (she had read Timothy Leary, too)—and she dropped out of the university. She did, however, continue dance and art classes at Cabrillo Community College.

That winter Elene moved downtown (farther from the university) into a tiny pink house on Broadway. There was space in the living room for an upright piano, and we had inherited a spinet from a friend. We shipped it to Elene at her new place. Now I had an added reason to feel good. I could think of her with music again, with Mozart sonatas and Chopin nocturnes.

She got a job as a busgirl at the Tea Cup Chinese restaurant on the Garden Mall, making $350 a month, including tips. But the job only lasted six months. The smell of deep-frying pork revolted her, and the dining room was full of cigarette smoke. She was now living for weeks at a time on sprouts and grasses and juices—carrot, broccoli, and apple. Wheatgrass became particularly important, and the Tea Cup with its pork grease and cigarette smoke didn't stand a chance against wheatgrass.

I was talking on the phone with my brother in Tucson. I mentioned that Elene had quit her job. He grumbled, "Cut off her funds and she'll keep jobs. What she needs is a bit of tough love." There was the old excess-indulgence guilt trip.

I hesitantly said into the phone, "I don't think cutting off money would faze her. She'd just eat less."

And I tried to explain to my brother how I now felt, how a job for Elene had become a ruthless cruelty. For her, unlike the rest of us, the prospect of doing another person's bidding when it contradicts your deepest beliefs is a bitter ordeal; if she had been an early Christian, she might have given her life for her beliefs. No job could stand in the way of her beliefs.

Elene came home for Christmas. On her first night the three of us were in the living room. Shirley and I were reading the paper; Elene was at the Knabe, playing a Rachmaninoff prelude. When it was over, she turned to us. "I don't think I told you that I moved out of the pink house."

Practical me, my mind switched right away to things. "What happened to the piano?"

"I lent it to friends. Don't worry, Papa. It's fine."

"Who are these friends? Students?"

"Oh, no. People I know on the mall. Don't worry, Papa. I don't believe in things. We have too many things. Things clutter up our lives. We have to unburden ourselves so our energies can flow. I have to purge all those medications I took. I'm into body work now."

She went on to elaborate on Rolfing and Lomi body work and polarity.

It was as if she were talking another language. I picked up on polarity. "Poles of what?"

"Energy, Papa. All our pains and emotional troubles come from an imbalance of energy currents. It's everything you eat and think; it's your total environment. It's manipulating your body so the energies flow right."

She went on. "It's so much better than the meds I took."

She proposed that she be trained in polarity, taking a seven-week course at the Polarity Institute on Mt. Shasta. It cost $1,000. She would get a certificate that would allow her to practice—giving massages, counseling on diet and lifestyles.

I felt as if riptides were pulling at my feet. I was losing my strength to resist. I knew there was something wrong, but I couldn't find the power to fight against the current.

I asked weakly, "Does the $1,000 include food and board?"

We read the brochures. We called the directors. Our negative feelings softened. And Elene went off to the Shasta Forest Lodge near Fall River Mills, a remote area that the brochures said was "known for its spiritual vibrations." She ate fresh fruits and vegetables, cold-pressed oil, sprouts, sunflower shoots, buckwheat lettuce, and wheatgrass. She learned the bones and muscles of the body and their manipulation; she practiced new yoga positions; she meditated, and she differentiated between "purifying diets and health-giving diets." In seven weeks she graduated as a Polarity Health Educator.

When Elene got back to Santa Cruz, she bought a massage table, had a flyer printed: *Elene, Certificated Polarity Health Educator*. Against a blue human figure surrounded by dotted circles representing outflowing energy were the words, *Polarity Balancing System, Clear Thinking, Energy Manipulations, Food Awareness, Polarity Yoga*. She began to attract clients at $10 an hour. It seemed she might have something going, and I thought, "Only in Santa Cruz."

The first time we heard about Homer Bresloff was in connection with polarity. "I had a new client today," Elene began on the phone. "He's very nice."

Shirley and I were both on the line, different phones. Shirley asked his name.

"Homer. I met him on the campus, drinking coffee. He took one of my cards. I gave him his first massage today. He asked me out. We're going to a concert on the campus."

I confess my mind was already bogged down in the picture of a young woman massaging the muscles of a half-naked young man. I was afraid to speak, afraid of what I might say. I let Shirley talk.

"What's he like?"

"He's an art major. I've seen him in classes. He's also a physics major. You'd like him, Papa."

In the weeks ahead we heard a lot about Homer. Concerts, picnics at the beach, walks in the redwoods, movies. In January she moved in with him, to his small house in Bonnie Doon, a wooded canyon just outside Santa Cruz.

"What's happening with your clients?" old worldly me asked.

"I can't stand the pressures of those appointments," she said. "I can't divorce myself from the troubles I hear. It's like I'm absorbing their damaged auras. I come out feeling ill."

"But a job's a job." I said. "Nobody likes everything about a job."

The waves were rolling again. What could I do? And the next call was the ninth wave, the biggest. "Papa, we're engaged to be married."

Oh, Good Lord! My daughter engaged. And to a man I'd never met. And it had begun with massaging muscles! Oh, Good Lord, help me! All I said was, "When?"

"Next summer. Homer wants to wait 'til he graduates in June. We're very happy."

I didn't have it in me to bluster. I said, "We have to meet Homer. Why don't you come down for a weekend?"

It was between terms and they agreed. We were to pick them up at the Greyhound station late Friday afternoon. I fear I was prepared to dislike him. I kept repeating those pictures of him lying on a massage table and Elene working over his arms and chest and stomach and legs. It seemed so wrong that he would let her do that. What kind of a man was he? I couldn't imagine letting Shirley do that to me when we had first met.

And when they stepped off the bus, he had a small beard and long sideburns. I never had liked a chin beard. Counterculture for sure, I thought. "Make love, not war." Probably why he added physics to his art major. Hoped that physics majors would get deferred. One way to get out of making war. And his art side played right into Elene's hands.

"Hi," he said. "Glad to meet you." He gave Shirley a hug.

That seemed pretty aggressive, I thought. He knows all the angles. And they were having their effect on Shirley. She was all smiles as he took Elene's arm and we headed for the car.

We ate at our favorite Italian restaurant. Homer wasn't the least bit bashful. He ordered a vegetarian cannelloni without asking what it was, as if he had had cannelloni all his life. He suggested Chianti and we asked him to choose a brand, which he did without hesitation.

Shirley got down to business and turned to Homer. "Tell us about your parents."

"Dad's an engineer. Mom takes care of the house. They live in Scarsdale, New York."

I had once had an aunt who lived in Scarsdale, and she was the rich one of the family. So at least there might be money somewhere in the background.

"Brothers? Sisters?" Shirley went on.

"No. I'm the only. Same with Elene, I know. Maybe that's why we like each other. Two spoiled brats wanting to spoil one another."

I wasn't exactly overjoyed at that picture.

"What are you going to do with your physics?" That was my question.

"Engineering, probably civil. My folks say they'll help me get through grad school."

"When you're married, we'd certainly want to help, too." Shirley was a little quick on that one, I thought. Of course, she didn't say how much. I guess it was safe enough for now.

"I'm going to keep painting though, and I hope Elene will, too. We both agree that modern art needs some help. We need to narrow the gap between impressionism and abstract expressionism. If you move too fast in artistic change, you lose your audience, and I'm not romantic enough to think that only the painter counts. Without someone watching, he's nothing—you know, like that sound in the forest with no one there."

God, I thought, he's going out of his way to impress us. But then he turned to me straight, smiled, and said, "Forgive me. I must sound like I'm trying to impress you. I didn't mean it that way."

Elene was grinning from ear to ear. She wasn't eating a bite of her dinner. She had stirred it a bit with her fork, but I knew she hadn't eaten anything. She asked for some herb tea and was careful to stipulate chamomile. It steeped for the rest of the meal, but she never poured any out to drink.

That night we showed him the room in the back where Michael had slept and we told Elene her room was ready for her. Elene said offhandedly, "I'll be with Homer."

Oh, will you! I thought.

"Don't frown, Papa. We're used to it."

The next day, Saturday, the two went off exploring. He wore shorts and in the sunlight as they got into the car I noticed his knees were well-formed, his legs straight, and he had good calf muscles.

Over a second cup of coffee in the kitchen, Shirley and I conferred.

Shirley said, "I like him."

"He's got a good mind, no doubt about that."

"Much more. He's thoughtful of her. I noticed it over and over."

"He comes on so strong."

"I don't see anything wrong with that."

I couldn't argue with her. But my mind was not calm. Was he real? What kind of a front was he putting up for us?

After dinner I lit a fire. Homer sat on the couch beside Elene, who suggested that he try my guitar. I dragged it out and wiped off the dust. He took it from the case gently, said, "It's a Martin," and beamed. He tuned it. He ran a few chords in F and F minor and then a scale in G. He smiled at Elene and began to sing.

"Sail, bonnie boat, like a bird on the wing..."

I loved that song—Bonnie Prince Charlie, the lad that's born to be king—"onward the sailors cry." I knew it was a favorite of Shirley's, too. His voice was clear and true, simple, not operatic, with a wide baritone range. When the waters raged with fury, his chords ripped in minor dissonance, then calmed again into major—"over the sea to Skye."

We didn't applaud. We sat almost entranced as he strummed into another key and went on. "Once I was a bachelor and I lived all alone..." How many times had I sung that without ever tiring of it? "...and I worked at the weaver's trade." When he came to "and the only, only thing that I did that was wrong was to woo a fair young maid," he looked at Elene and smiled. I kept humming with him, then in the third chorus, "She reminds me of the summertime..." I burst into song, too, and Homer immediately switched into harmony. "...Was to keep her from the foggy, foggy dew." We weren't bad, there in the firelight, dispelling the foggy, foggy dew of England. Shirley clapped and we all laughed.

He kept strumming, moving into a minor key, playing with chords until he began, "Oh, who will tie thy shoe, and who will glove thy hand..." Now he was looking at Elene. "And who will kiss those ruby lips, when I am gone?...I'm goin' away, but I'm comin' back, though it were ten thousand mile."

It seems ridiculous, but my doubts about Homer seemed to be crumbling. What I had seen as arrogance began to look like assurance. Egotism became responsibility. Intellectualism became intelligence. Had he sung his way into acceptance? My thoughts were not wholly unrealistic. If Elene's mind became troubled again, he could calm her with a song. How much better than Haldol! And what could be the side effects? No more than the warmth of a smile or a kiss on ruby lips. I could even now begin to imagine them married.

When they returned to Santa Cruz, Homer sent us a thank-you letter. He concluded, "I love Elene incredibly and I want to take care of her so that we may grow together in the loving space that we create."

As Shirley read the letter to me, her voice was breaking. "I don't think Elizabeth Barrett Browning wrote anything as lovely," she said.

"I wonder if he knows about Elene's emotional problems? I didn't mention it."

Shirley answered. "I did. That last night. He was aware of her hospitalizations. He said she had told him all about them. They didn't make the slightest difference to him. He was ready and anxious to help her find stability."

Homer's parents were understandably anxious to meet their only son's prospective bride. They planned a trip to Santa Cruz in March. Elene and Homer suggested that we come up at the same time to meet our in-laws-to-be. Some demon in me wished they would just go off and get married with a minimum of pressure on Elene. But what could we say but "sure" to the March gathering?

When the weekend came, Homer and Elene picked us up at the San Jose airport. Elene was in an Indian bedspread sari with her hair cascading down her back. She said almost nothing on the drive back to Santa Cruz.

Homer explained, "My folks found a funky little motel up in the redwoods. You can stay there, too, if you want."

"That would be fine." So we began in the tow of the Bresloffs. The motel consisted of isolated cabins with cold linoleum floors and gas-panel heat. There were not even paved walks between the cabins, only the spongy carpet from the canopy of redwoods.

We met Mrs. Bresloff on that brown carpet outside our cabin. Homer had brought her over while his father was showering. She wore a silk flowered dress and pantyhose with moderately high-heeled shoes. (Shirley had on slacks and canvas shoes.)

Ida Bresloff was clearly used to being in charge. "We've reserved dinner tomorrow at the Brookside, which Homer says is the best. It'll be our celebration."

The next night we were to meet at Homer and Elene's place in Bonnie Doon at six. Don Bresloff drove the four of us from the motel. When we drove up the dirt road, Homer was waiting outside. "All of you come in," he said. "Elene isn't ready and we can have a glass of wine."

We all traipsed in. The house was filled with plants. The furniture was sparse. Homer poured Chardonnay. "Elene should be ready soon," he said.

For about fifteen minutes the conversation roamed idly.

Homer refilled our glasses. A half hour went by, then forty-five minutes. No Elene.

"We're going to miss our reservation," Don Bresloff said.

"I'll call them." And Homer disappeared. We could hear his voice with Elene's. But we couldn't make out the words.

After almost an hour, Elene appeared. I hardly recognized her. She wore a skirt and long drooping blouse, untucked, which went almost to her knees. She had on pantyhose and Birkenstock sandals. Her hair was done in braids on the top of her head. I envisioned her working on those braids all the time we were waiting. Elene said nothing about her not being ready.

At the restaurant we had toasts to the couple, and things were becoming more festive. We ordered rack of lamb and salmon and trout, and when it came to Elene, she shook her head.

"Nothing."

"Nothing?" I said. "There're plenty of vegetarian items."

"I'll have some tea."

When the food came, I was terribly embarrassed for her. The rest of us were gorging on this celebratory meal and she was eating nothing. Nor did she speak much. She sat in long periods of silence, just smiling.

"What classes are you taking now?" Ida Bresloff asked her.

"The environment is all mixed up, you know. So many toxic exhalations. Destruction."

Ida Bresloff countered, "You don't really believe that, do you?"

Elene said simply, "Destruction," and sank back into silence.

Homer said, "There're lots of problems in this world, Mom."

"Yes," Ida Bresloff said, and looked straight at her son as if to say, and we have some right here.

During dessert Elene began to talk compulsively. Subjects overflowed onto one another. Wheatgrass was superimposed on nuclear horror, third-world poverty was equated with vegetarianism, and racism was related to magnetic auras. I could follow somewhat because I knew Elene. I was sure that Ida Bresloff was imagining a junkyard of the counterculture. She only nodded, looked occasionally at her husband, and smiled faintly.

I don't know how we got through that evening. It was not unlike pain seeping slowly from a tooth.

The next morning Homer and his father drove us to the airport. Homer drove with Shirley beside him; Don and I sat in back. I took the chance to let Don know that we intended to help them get through Homer's graduate school.

"We do, too," he answered. "Homer'll make it fine." I noticed he was careful to avoid "they."

For the next two weeks Shirley and I didn't talk much about the night at Brookside. I guess we assumed or hoped that things weren't as bad as we had imagined. The Bresloffs might understand the tensions young people feel.

Then we had a collect call from Elene. Her first comment was, "This will be expensive. I'm calling from Hawaii."

"Hawaii!"

"I came here with my rent money. One-way ticket. I'm fine."

"Is Homer with you?"

"I don't know where Homer is."

It was like a dull thud. My heart jumped into my mouth. It was as we had feared.

"You've broken up?"

"I don't know what you call it. I don't want to talk about it. I like it here."

"Where do you sleep?"

"I'm in a health food store right now. There're lots of people here like me."

I had no trouble picturing those people. We had seen them in every commune we had visited—smiling, grimy-shirted, brimming with impossible ideals, in this case living off the land, taking manna from heaven, and sleeping like foxes in whatever hole came along. I didn't like the picture, especially when it included Elene.

"Do you want a ticket home?"

Her voice choked up a bit. "Yes. I'd like that. My wallet got stolen out of my backpack." So much for the counterculture.

She wanted to go back to Santa Cruz. We used our credit card to buy her one-way ticket with United and had it held for her.

After putting down the phone, I said to Shirley, "Ida Bresloff gets what she wants, and you can be sure Elene is not what she wanted."

"It must hurt Elene, really hurt. We've got to go up to see her."

The next week we drove to Santa Cruz. All the way up I kept thinking of Homer. He had grown so in my mind that I saw in him the kind of person I dreamed of for Elene—a talented, promising young man, willing to work with Elene because he loved her, sympathizing with her moods, protecting her from stress, and able to provide the resources necessary to smooth her path. Now she was adrift again, adrift in Santa Cruz.

Chapter Seven

Better with Sprouts

It was the fall of 1978. Patches of fog laced the highway from Moss Landing to Aptos, and then cleared as we pulled into Santa Cruz. We checked in at the motel, and took off right away to find Elene's new address on Spruce Street. It was a small yellow house tucked behind a large gray Victorian. The driveway harbored a couple of motorcycles and a splotchy Volkswagen. We parked on the street and walked back. On the three steps to Elene's door a couple of women in shorts and halters sat with hair over their faces, drying in the sun.

"Is Elene here?"

One woman threw back her hair. "Think she's inside. You her parents? Glad to meet you." And she smiled.

That was pleasant, but I thought, who are you?

There was no need to knock. No knock could be heard over the decibels of rock that came from inside. We walked in. We could see three men stretched on futons in the front room and a man and a woman in dark glasses seated on the floor of the hall, smoking what smelled like marijuana. The woman had one hand on a guitar beside her but wasn't playing it.

We found Elene in the kitchen stuffing clumps of greens into the juicer, which made a whine that almost obscured the clangor of the music from the other room.

She saw us. "Oh, you're here. I have to finish this job."

Shirley went over to offer help and give her a bag of artichokes we had bought in Castroville. I drifted back into the hall. The man there got up and put out his hand. "You must be Elene's father. I'm Al. Glad to meet you." I shook his hand, which was sticky.

Al said, "You had a good trip?"

"Very good. Where you from?"

"Evanston, Illinois. I came from a jail school to a real school."

What in the world did that mean? I asked, "Are you at the university here?"

"Hell, no. The school of life."

So we had come to the school of life. "Where did you meet Elene?"

"Grapevine said her place was good for camping out. Living in."

Great, I thought. We're not only in the school of life; we're on the grapevine. "Do you eat here?"

"We all bring stuff. It's like a communal table."

"Do you all help with the rent?" I knew it was a stupid question, but I liked the snide dig it made.

"Would if I could. I don't have any money."

He had three books on the floor and he reached down to pick them up. I noticed two titles—William Blake's *Songs of Innocence* and Allen Ginsberg's *Howl*.

I asked him if he was into poetry.

"Sure. We read it together at night."

Shirley and Elene came along. Elene smiled at Al, who melted away. When I looked at Elene close, my ire began to mount. Even my terribly weak vision could tell she was gaunt. She wore her usual Indian bedspread sari. Her hair streamed down her back but it had not been brushed or combed.

"Who are all these people?"

"Friends. They stay with me."

"You're only back from Hawaii two weeks."

"I think they knew this house before."

"So why do you let them stay?"

"They're all right. They're friends."

I opened up without thinking. "They're leeches," I said. "They're living off your food and rent."

"I don't like you saying that."

Shirley interjected, "Let's not argue."

Elene turned on Shirley. "Why not? Arguing is good for you. You ought to do more of it."

Saying that to Shirley made me see red. "Let's get out of here, Shirley." And I said to Elene, "We'll pick you up for dinner, about six thirty. Do you have a watch?"

"I can even read it," said Elene, and she turned back into the kitchen.

When we came at six thirty, Elene was not there. Some bleary-eyed male in fringed shorts and tie-dyed T-shirt told us, "She went off with George."

So Shirley and I went off to Nature's Harvest and ordered scrambled tofu.

"We've lost her to the drug culture," I said.

"The culture, maybe. Elene, no." Shirley answered. "I watched her closely in the kitchen. Eating the artichokes. Her eyes were not dilated in the least. She wasn't shaking. She told me she was sorry her friends were into drugs, though she guessed they took them every night. I don't think she would abuse her body like that. We may not like all that wheatgrass stuff, but I think it's saved her from drugs."

"But she's surrounded with terrible temptations. We've got to get her out of that place."

"You forget how strong her will is. She's a woman with a will of iron."

The next morning we got to Elene's about ten. She was in the kitchen juicing oranges and apples. The rest of the house was a shambles of sleeping bodies, crumpled clothes, and dirty dishes.

A man was with Elene in the kitchen drinking the orange juice as she poured it.

"I'm Robert Hine," I said, reaching out my hand.

He took it weakly. "Karma," he said in almost a whisper. I guessed he meant his name was Karma, but I wasn't sure and I decided not to ask.

He wore ragged jeans and a jacket with blotches of paint. His hair was long and a beard covered most of his face. His eyes were almost lost in hair.

Elene said nothing about last night, and I decided to forget it, too.

"Can Karma come to lunch with us?"

"Of course," we said together.

"I'm going to the fairgrounds." He smiled at us sheepishly and turned back to her in his whispering voice. He walked over to a contraption in the corner of the kitchen. He threw the straps over his shoulders and tied another around his waist. In front of him then was a plastic-covered tray filled with bags of popcorn. His two hands could work freely inside the plastic cover. He brushed by us with a "So long" and was gone.

By then it was midday. The three of us went off to the organic produce market. We stood in front of a case of Gravenstein apples. "Let's get these," I offered.

Elene looked blankly at the case. There were others around— Red Delicious, Granny Smiths. Elene was looking at each. "I can't decide."

"Why?"

"Which is from the best environment?"

"They're all organic. Isn't that enough to know?"

"I can't decide."

It was that way with every crate—carrots, chard, tomatoes. It was as if these were the last vegetables we were ever going to buy and the salvation of the earth depended on her choice. We must have been in the market for two hours. By the time we took the crates home, it was four o'clock and our proposed late lunch had become an early supper.

Kareem Jo's was an upscale, white-tablecloth place. When we were seated, I started the conversation.

"Karma seemed like a good person," I ventured.

"Why do you use that word *good*?"

"I don't know. Just a general term."

"I don't like it. It's you sitting in judgment."

"We make judgments all the time."

"I know. I make charts of them. Every time I make a judgment I list it. There are spatial judgments and there are linear judgments. I'm into spatial judgments, and you make linear judgments."

"What does that mean?"

"You use rulers on everything. Energy fits into space. Space is the ultimate environment. That's where space is. You can't put rulers to energy."

Elene had ordered an avocado curry salad. It looked delicious but she hadn't taken a bite, only kept talking. After we had nearly finished our soup and salad, Shirley spooned a piece of avocado into Elene's mouth, and she chewed it and swallowed without stopping talking. She was like an automaton that wasn't at all aware of her immediate surroundings. Space and the total environment were now her dwelling place. "Space is where we live. Space has nothing to do with rulers."

Shirley forked a piece of tomato into Elene's mouth. She swallowed it and then suddenly realized what had happened. "Why are you feeding me? What do you think I am?"

She jumped up and ran through the tables, saying, "You don't know I live in space," and soon she was out the front door of the restaurant. Shirley ran after her. I stayed behind and paid the bill.

I had noticed which way they had gone, so I followed up the street. I found them on a bus bench two blocks away—Elene crying, Shirley's arm around her.

"I'll stay with Elene if you get the car," I said.

"You use rulers," Elene said to me, her tears over.

"Maybe I can change."

"I don't think so."

"Are you taking your meds?" I don't know how I was brave enough to ask, but I badly wanted to know.

"Rulers. Of course not. I'll never take those meds again."

When we were all in the car, I asked Shirley to drive us up the coast a bit where we could watch the sea. By then the winter sun was setting.

Shirley was cold and stayed in the car. Elene and I leaned on a rail at the edge of the cliff looking over the breakers to a glorious sunset.

"Stare into the light, Papa. Don't blink. Just stare. Let it flow into your whole body. Let it be absorbed by your aura."

I did. And the color throbbed inside me. I did blink, however. I looked back at her eyes—the reds and yellows of the sun reflected in the black center and the hazel-green pupils. It was beautiful, she was beautiful, and I loved her.

That night Shirley and I talked long and hard. How could we get her out of that house? Shirley wasn't sure we wanted to. "At least she's seeing people, not hiding in a bedroom."

"Do you suppose it's us that bring on the phobias? If we stay here long, I know I'll get in an argument with her so-called friends. They're leeching on her."

We went over in the morning to say good-bye, claiming we had to get back. Elene said she loved us and gave us big hugs. But I was convinced she was relieved at our going.

So, drenched in apprehension and helplessness, we drove the dreary route south. This time we said almost nothing for the first fifty miles, each sorting out our feelings. If Elene was truly mentally ill, what was our role in her life? I felt little control over a child I loved. I was no longer a director. I was an observer. Our parenthood had been replaced by a society that seemed strangely foreign.

In a way I felt relieved. We hadn't done that good a job with Elene, and now the county of Santa Cruz with the help of the federal government was standing in for us. The police had seemed kind to her, the mental health facilities were as good as they come—far better than any we had seen in the Riverside area—and the federal SSI program stood by to foot much of the bill. We had become the fifth wheel. Was that where we belonged?

Shirley's steady driving was like a medieval chant, consoling and compassionate, the rhythmic rows of onions and lettuce beckoning toward serenity. Santa Maria, San Luis Obispo, and Santa Barbara brought us closer and closer to our own lives in contrast with Elene's. The tedium of Los Angeles and the Pomona Freeway pulled down further the screen that separated us from the yellow house on Spruce Street with its sweet smell of marijuana.

Our lives at home were full. Shirley was learning computer programming, littering the house with great cartons of punched cards. She volunteered at Head Start. She had numberless friends. I was coping with my emerging blindness. My vision was about 20:400 corrected, but I knew it would get worse, so I was learning Grade Three Braille, a shorthand version. I lectured using Braille notes. I brailled three-by-five cards and tucked them in my coat, nonchalantly pocketing a hand to surreptitiously read the notes. In my office daily readers kept me up on obscure literature. I was using a talking computer for writing, and was nearly finished with a manuscript about community in the American West, including a final chapter on the current communes.

Even with all this activity, I cannot claim that the screen between us and Santa Cruz was that opaque. There was scarcely an hour in which my thoughts, and I think Shirley's too, didn't return to Elene. Shirley had a few close friends with whom she talked about Elene, and I was open with my brother and sister. But that was not always easy because most of our friends and relatives gave us the feeling that we were carrying the burden too far and assuming too much responsibility. The result was that we often kept silent about Elene and sealed off that portion of our lives. There was a quiet comfort in assuming that we shared a separate space with Elene and few, if any, others were fully privy to it.

A month later we had a call from a social worker. Elene had been admitted to the Santa Cruz County mental health unit. They gave us no further details. I called to cancel my Friday class; we booked a flight for the next morning and flew up. We found Elene in the wood-frame building, the one we remembered. We were taken through the one locked door and seated in the patients' living area right beside the dining tables. Patients wandered around, some talking to themselves, others arguing with staff. A call came for "groups" and they dribbled off to various other rooms.

Elene came down the hall. My heart fell. She was shuffling, and her first words were slurred. I filled in the rest of the picture—blurry vision, zombie eyes, trembling. She said little. We covered our feelings and stuttered on about home and people she knew. She said she hated the cramps. The doctor had told her he would give her something for the side effects, but he hadn't yet.

We were there for scarcely half an hour when Karma was ushered in, carrying an enormous armload of red floribunda roses. He grinned at us and gave the roses to Elene. She put them down on the chair beside her. "Where did you get them?" she asked.

"Growing over a fence." He grinned again.

Maybe it was time for us to go, I thought. "Can we bring you something from your house?" I asked her.

She thought for a minute. "A sweater, I guess. If you can find my blue one. And toothpaste, the organic. They don't use it here."

"We'll be back this evening." And we left the two of them. They were saying nothing; they only sat looking at each other, then looking away.

When we got to Elene's yellow house, Shirley left me in the living room while she went into the back rooms to find Elene's sweater and toothpaste. The front room held a scattering of people. A man and a woman lay on the couch lazily embracing. The man closest to me wore mirrored dark glasses though the room was dark, and somehow those mirrored glasses set up my hackles.

"What's your name?" I asked him.

"Star."

"Star what?"

"Star in the sky."

"I know where stars are, but what's your name?"

"I told you, Star."

"How do you know Elene?"

"Well, man, I don't really know Elene. I heard her place was cool."

"So you're just living off her rent and gas and electricity, probably eating her food?"

"Come on, man, don't be so uptight. I'm not the only one."

An inexplicable rage shook me like a freak storm. I was mad. I was mad at life for doing what it was doing to Elene. I was mad at the medications for torturing her. I was mad at these drifting kids. I was mad at this particular one for his mirrored dark glasses that made him look blind when I knew he wasn't. I probably was mad, too, because those glasses reflected my own coming blindness. I started raising my voice and it cracked. "I think you'd better get out of here."

"Yeah, I won't be here more than a few more days. Gotta hit the road."

"No, I mean now. Right now. I want to see you out of here."

"Jeez, man, you're so uptight."

The others in the room were very quiet, listening to us. I turned to them all. "I want you all out of here. Elene is in the hospital and I want you all out of here."

The others began to mumble. I heard the words anal retentive whispered. I couldn't see well enough what they were doing, but I felt a vague unease. There were four young men in the room who could easily have knocked me around, thrown me out. I was, after all, threatening their communal life. It made me think of days with Shirley in communes where the young ones were running around naked, smoking pot, jumping into the hot tub, and telling me to follow. I never did but I often feared vaguely that they were about to pull me in.

These men were not threatening, though, and I was incensed enough not to care. I kicked one duffel bag toward the door. It was a childish gesture, but I felt childish, blaming these kids for wanting to live in a counterculture. Childish or not, I blamed them.

A woman in a flimsy shirt without a bra, seeing me kick the duffel, called, "Wait up, sir, that's mine."

"Get it out of here."

"Sorry you're so upset." She came over and put her hand on my sleeve.

She was sweet. My voice fell. "I just want this house cleared. OK?"

"I'll round the people up for you. I love Elene."

Shirley came in. "I can't find the blue sweater, but I found a beige one. And I have the toothpaste. Shall we go?"

When we were alone I told Shirley I had lost my temper and yelled the whole bunch out of there. She laughed. "I could hear you from the other room. I think you scared them."

"I did?"

"Just remember it's Elene's choice to live that way." Then she sighed. "It wouldn't be so if Homer were still around. Maybe Elene wouldn't even be in the hospital."

We talked with the hospital psychiatrist, but learned little. He used vague terms like *psychotic*. I asked if he suspected schizophrenia. He said schizophrenia is a complicated disease, maybe several illnesses like cancer. It involves at least three elements: disturbances in thinking such as speaking illogically with discontinuities and irrelevancies; disturbances in emotion such as inappropriate outbursts and fears; and disturbances in perception like delusions and hallucinations. Elene, he said, exhibits bizarre behavior, probably fulfilling the first two elements, but she was not at the moment having hallucinations. So he would not diagnose schizophrenia, at least not yet. His reluctance, he admitted, was partly based on his belief that schizophrenia was not a single illness, but many. And that, he bemoaned, makes all diagnosis slippery.

He did tell us more about the circumstances leading to Elene's hospitalization. The police had been called. They found her lying in a fetal position in the crosswalk of a street where it entered the Pacific Garden mall. They had carried her to the sidewalk.

"She didn't talk or move," he said. "The police brought her here. Since we had a file on her, her admission was easy and we got a seventy-two-hour hold from the court. That made medication possible."

I interrupted, "I know you have her history, and I assume you know she's miserable with Haldol."

"Of course. We'll do everything we can to medicate the side effects. And we know she's anxious to get out. That's typical. In a week or two she should be stable and can go to SART."

"I don't know that word. What is SART?"

"Sub-acute Rehabilitation Treatment. It's a good facility, pleasant. Good people there."

I wasn't that happy with this doctor. Why should he resist the schizophrenia diagnosis? She had had hallucinations in the past if not now, and many of her ideas verged on delusions. Why not call a spade a spade?

Shirley was more understanding. "It's a slippery field," she said to me. "I can't blame them for stepping cautiously."

We returned to Santa Cruz after Elene had been moved to SART. We found SART on a street of small bungalows with maybe forty patients in two long, one-story buildings overlooking an arroyo with eucalyptus. I liked the place. We found there a relaxed air of freedom with people sitting on the grass or playing ping-pong. We knew, though, that our hope, not our reason, was speaking to us. Inside those walls we knew well enough to expect frantic eyes, complicated tensions, and worried supervisors. We were only thinking of Elene, and she seemed infinitely better, certainly better enough to come to a relaxed place like this.

She had work assignments interspersed with therapy sessions. After a given number of cooperative hours, she could earn day passes for visits into the city, usually accompanied by staff members or, we would learn, by us.

I had once read that the ancient Greeks handled madness by sending the person to a quiet island, far from all the distractions of the world, where a peaceful life could restore them. Was it too much to hope that SART would be that kind of therapy for Elene?

She was assigned a social worker, Tim Woods, a man in his late thirties, with a small, clipped beard and a ponytail. We liked him instinctively. He and Elene seemed to get along well. He was a dedicated person who had made his peace with the world. He and Elene laughed a lot together, and I felt good just seeing them.

So when the time came to sail home on the highway, there was a new upbeat rhythm in the serried rows of broccoli.

When Elene was restored to her yellow house, it was empty. She wouldn't say on the phone how many of her things had gone out in those duffel bags. "Papa, I miss the people not the things. They don't steal; they borrow. If I give them a sweater now, they give me one when I need it. What's wrong with that?"

"Nothing, I guess, unless you can't find the people when you need the sweater."

"I'm reading Anaïs Nin and Henry Miller. We're all too tied up with material objects. I believe in divesting ourselves. A simple life is the best life."

She was making sense, at least countercultural sense. I couldn't deny that and I was grateful. But I mourned for the spinet piano, given away to God knows whom.

I sat down after dinner to write.

Dear Elene,

Isn't it true that you need more continuity in your life, more feeling that what has gone on in the past is still going on and can be a kind of anchor for you? Sometimes this feeling can come through things, little gifts or objects that recall other times and places and people. Or a book that you have once loved. Or a plant. You don't have to make a fetish of things or attach yourself too strongly to them. But they are symbols and remembrances, and I frankly think Anaïs Nin and Henry Miller are wrong in saying otherwise. And I'll bet that even they would claim a few books or letters or sentimental gifts are important in their lives.

All of which leads me to think that you've stripped your life too clean of things. Maybe you can gradually get back—can I use the word re-collect?—some of them, some of the things that have been lent out and which the borrowers would not mind giving back. Your piano maybe? A chair? A book or two?

I love you so much. We care so much. Our lives have been so enriched by you and all that you have meant to us that you must bear with our love and caring, which so often gets expressed in advice. But think about it and love us in return.

Papa

We never heard back on that one, but on the phone we could tell that things weren't going too well at the yellow house. We didn't pursue the feeling because we were trying to rearrange our own lives. With my vision dimming so, we had found it harder and harder to keep up with the trials of our old dream house. The plumbing stopped up every Christmas Eve. The orange trees grew scale like fish in spite of poisonous spray applied in clouds twice a year. The roof was beginning to leak. We couldn't cope with it all and decided to exchange the house for a condominium out on Victoria Avenue. So we sold and moved into a pleasant place with a small extra bedroom and no outside upkeep. Our dream house faded into the past and we often drove by it with the sad eyes of memory.

We broke the news to Elene gently. Whatever happened, she said, the old house would be her house. But her main thoughts had turned in another direction. She had read in *Prevention* an ad for Great Oaks, a farm commune run by a psychiatrist and his nurse wife in isolated country abutting a national forest south of Eugene, Oregon.

Shirley was her usual upbeat self. "How many times have we said that Elene needs a place with minimal pressures, no TVs or microwaves? Life on a farm with the support of a few caring vegetarians sounds like a perfect solution." She read the Great Oaks literature with a new song in her heart.

I called the director. "What do you mean when you say you live communally?"

"We ask everyone to pay $1,000 a month. But you can work in the kitchen, in the garden, cleaning, whatever, and get $6.00 an hour toward that $1,000. So if Elene works 180 hours a month, she's done her share."

"She may not be able to do that at first."

"People often need time to adjust to our ways. We understand that."

I wasn't willing to trust the pictures on the brochure so I called Bingham, a friend I knew at the University of Oregon, and he happily drove out to Great Oaks and reported that it was not posh, that it looked like a commune—Volkswagen Beetles and goats—but that it seemed well run and reasonably clean.

So, leaning on our shadowy and spidery hopes, stifling our grinding fears, we bought Elene, fragile as an eggshell, a one-way ticket for a direct flight to Eugene where the Great Oaks people had agreed to pick her up. Much later a woman at Great Oaks told us how frightened Elene seemed when she arrived there, shaking and frowning.

Elene stayed at Great Oaks for six months. It was a farm bordering a forest. A big garden produced most of their food. They raised a few sheep from which they clipped wool for spinning and weaving. The director thought the best therapy was small groups taking long walks through the woods. And we imagined Elene hiking with young people in the late summer warmth and the blazing fall.

For their cooperative work there was a training period during which they did not get full recompense, but after a few months, Elene received full pay, reducing our monthly fees.

The holidays loomed. She did not want to come home for Thanksgiving or Christmas. She preferred the quiet around the Great Oaks Christmas tree. We even noticed she talked of exchanging gifts. But they were to be simple, homemade gifts.

Shirley and I concluded that she had found her place in the sun—a rural spot, close to nature, not too far from culture in Eugene, but isolated from the pressures of crowded cities. Perhaps in time she would learn to make a simple living, engage in arts and crafts, and find some kindred soul to settle down with.

In January we were jolted back into another reality. Her phone call was from Santa Cruz.

"Took the Grey Rabbit from Eugene. Know about the Grey Rabbit?"

"You don't mean the Greyhound?"

"No. The Grey Rabbit is a co-op run by students. It costs almost nothing compared."

"Have you left Great Oaks?"

"Yes. I couldn't take Oregon. Life was too slow."

My thoughts flashed back to London, when Shirley and I walked too slowly.

"We thought you liked it."

"I missed Santa Cruz, the coffee houses, the health food stores, the community events."

Was this the agoraphobic woman who couldn't face a bus or a market? I suspect my mouth was ajar.

We hurried up to Santa Cruz and found her in a small room in a big house. All she had to her name, except for the few clothes from Great Oaks, were a mug and a plate. We noticed right away that in the room across the hall lived Karma, the popcorn seller.

Elene was wearing a wide-brimmed hat, everywhere, inside and out. She did not look the blooming farm girl we had pictured at Great Oaks. Her conversation rambled. One minute she was talking about nuclear destruction and armaments, the next about microwaves and smoke alarms destroying the environment. When we took her out to Nature's Harvest for dinner, she looked into my eyes and declared me cured. "You can see now," she said. "Your aura is much clearer."

I did not pursue the matter.

We were able to get her to her mental health counselor, Tim Woods, and he talked with her at length. He took us aside afterward and said there was nothing he could do, that she did not pose a threat to herself or anyone else, that she was an independent adult over whom neither he nor we had any jurisdiction.

So we drove back to Riverside, saying little to the wind that blew down the Salinas Valley. Shirley and I knew we shared that leaden feeling in our stomachs; we again felt helpless. We wished we could do something. We sensed what would come next.

Within two weeks the Santa Cruz police called saying they had hospitalized Elene. She had been picked up walking naked through downtown Santa Cruz streets while she was having her period, bleeding profusely.

My mind burst with that horrible picture. Walking naked, paying no attention to her period! My little girl! What a nightmare to etch into my soul. I should be there with soft blankets and warm, wet cloths. Could I turn away those strangers staring at the lovely landscape of her body? At least it had been night. Did she feel protected by the night—the night protecting her in place of me?

In a knee-jerk reaction, we flew up, rented a car, and sped right away to the mental health unit of Dominican. We were getting to know the people, the nurses, the social workers. I blessed their familiar faces. Suzanne seemed particularly solicitous, and when the doctor told us later that Elene had bitten Suzanne when she had first been brought in, I could hardly believe how kind and forgiving the nurse had been.

Elene was now on medication. The side effects were not nearly as extreme. We didn't talk about the circumstances, the nakedness, the period. Her little spartan room seemed so neat and clean. Maybe she had forgotten the whole incident.

The psychiatrist expected her to be stable in a week or so and then released to SART again. We asked him our big question. "What is our role? What can we best do to help?"

"Your role is an important one," he said, "but it's a simple one. She must always feel that you're there. It doesn't have to be physically there beside her. Even being there by means of the phone can do it. She must always have the feeling that someone out there loves her and cares. Too many of my patients don't have that support. After five, six, or seven hospitalizations, parents often feel burned out, helpless, rejected, and they slowly drift away. If you want to help Elene, don't drift away."

The psychiatrist was in general a good prognosticator. But this time another factor entered—the patient advocate. In mental hospitals, they are usually there to see that patients are not held, medicated, or otherwise restrained unduly. Back at home, we learned from Elene that her patient advocate had talked with her and arranged to take her to her seventy-two-hour hearing before a judge. The advocate borrowed clothes for Elene from other patients. Karma was alerted and brought three of the gang who had once lived in the yellow house. They assured the judge that they could provide Elene with a place to live and they would vouch for her safety. The judge was sympathetic, seeing this neatly dressed woman speaking in her own defense and with friends to testify for her. He probably was quite aware of the demands on the county facilities, and would be happy to find good reasons to grant her release. And that's the way it worked. She was then free to go, free to stop her medications, free, as I feared, to resume the sad cycle.

The next summer—it was 1981—the cycle was dramatically interrupted. Elene called.

"I want to talk with Mom," she told me in a soft voice.

When Shirley got on the phone, I heard "Oh, dear" and "How many months," and I knew Elene was pregnant. It was one of those fears that we had repeatedly pushed deep under the pile. Now it had materialized. Here it was, staring us in the face. Shirley was staring straight back at the fear.

"Who is the father?" And then before long I heard, "Have you considered an abortion?"

Shirley was quiet for a long time, listening.

I went off to the kitchen. The pain twisted like a roiling current. I put on some hot water for coffee. I stared out the window. I felt numb.

Shirley soon came. "I guess you understood?"

"Who's the father?"

"Karma, of course."

"God. No income. No future. What'd she say about an abortion?"

"No chance whatever. She's ruled that out. She says she went that way once and she'll never do it again. Can you believe it, she remembers and hates what we thought was nothing to her. She says there are no doubts in her mind and no room for us to talk about it."

"Will he marry her?"

"I didn't ask that. Do we want them to get married?"

"She can't cope with a child alone."

"But I don't think he's right for her."

"A child needs a father, no matter."

"I suppose we could help raise it."

Now my voice did raise and crack. "Come on, Shirley. Cut it out. We're too old, and I'm basically blind, and your hands are full. I hate that. I hate it all. But that's the way it is. If Elene has no room to talk about abortion, we sure have no room to talk about raising another baby."

I continued to feel that the child needed a father and a name. Shirley leaned on the hope that she might find the right husband later.

"Come on, Shirley. An emotionally unstable woman with a child can't hope to find a man. And she loves Karma. I vote for marriage."

Shirley was stubborn. "A child needs the right father." She emphasized the word *right*.

I don't know why we argued like that. We weren't going to have the slightest say in their decision. In fact, we knew that pressure from us would probably have negative results.

Elene made the decision for marriage. I think she worried about raising a child alone. I think she wanted to have a secure father, and I think she had genuine feelings for Karma. She liked the idea of Karma's legal name, Daniel Carlson, on the birth certificate. So on November 7, 1981, Elene married Daniel Carlson in a redwood grove on the campus of the university. The ceremony was performed by Joseph Wortsberg, ThD, who called himself a "Christian minister"; and we never learned precisely what that meant. The only other people present were two witness-friends from the yellow house. Elene said the friends were into spiritual movements, and they wove garlands of wildflowers for the bride and groom.

Elene sent us the marriage certificate, which substituted for our being there. But I must say it hurt not to have been asked. I think it hurt Shirley more than me, because I was just glad they had decided on marriage, and I remembered how the pressures of parental presence had disrupted the Homer relationship. Better to get a license, take some kind of minister into a redwood grove and with wildflowers in hand and hair, say I do.

A few weeks later, the newlyweds came down to Riverside for Thanksgiving. Karma was a real contrast to Homer, much harder to talk with, a practical, hard-bitten loner. His parents were divorced, somewhere in Texas. He seldom contacted his mother. He was not a "school" person, though he had tried a community college with jobs in mind. This was the man I had campaigned to marry Elene. This was my son-in-law.

Rather than talk, he and Shirley worked a huge jigsaw puzzle of a tabby cat.

In our small kitchen, Shirley cooked a big turkey with cornbread stuffing, mashed sweet potatoes, white potatoes, peas, creamed spinach, and pumpkin pie. Karma seemed grateful enough, but it was not always easy to tell.

The next day we took a picnic to Palomar State Park. It was a cold day, and the park was desolate. Huddled around the picnic table, we spread out Shirley's food—potato salad with yogurt dressing, pickles, sliced apples, and, of course, turkey sandwiches with lettuce on whole grain bread. Shirley asked Karma if he liked the sandwiches.

"They'd be better with sprouts," he said.

Chapter Eight

The Golden Voyage

So our little girl was pregnant and determined to bear the child! Maybe somewhere deep in me was an adoptive father's tinge of regret that it wasn't my bloodline being prolonged, but I doubt it. Our chief emotions were wrapped in love and concern. What were the connections between mental stability and pregnancy? What happens if Elene needs the mental hospital or medications? We rummaged through the literature and found some reassurance that pregnancy usually has little lasting effect on the mental stability of the mother. That was good news, but there were also highly personal questions. How, for example, would Elene react to my inability to see her child?

Sometimes we reasoned that nursing a baby might exert a calming power. On the other hand, how about the lack of sleep? And what happens in later years when crises occur, like chicken-pox and measles? And how much does a child need consistent discipline, which might be in short supply?

Spock reminded us that a child is raised not by parents alone but by society at large, by relatives, friends, and schools. That was a hopeful thought, but even so, our worries usually outweighed it.

Meanwhile Elene and Karma had found a low-rent apartment a half block from the Pacific Garden Mall. It was on the roof, up long stairs above the kitchen of a restaurant.

In this apartment Elene wanted her baby to be born. She didn't trust hospitals. She was convinced they injected newborns with medicines that she considered poisons. She said seriously, "They circumcise little boys without ever asking the mother. They'd anesthetize me and I don't know what they might do then. They might tie my tubes. I won't have anything to do with hospitals. I want to give birth at home with a midwife. I'd like Karen Laing."

There was clearly little room for argument. Close the books on hospitals. Open a new book, a new facet of my education, the world of midwives.

We learned that the midwife movement was growing rapidly nationwide, and that one of its most respected leaders was Karen Laing in Santa Cruz. We called and talked with her. Her voice was strong and reassuring. She told us she was an RN and that she respected doctors. She was associated with one whom she could call at any moment in case of emergencies. She had performed over a hundred births and only once during a difficult breech birth had she needed to call the doctor and get the mother to the hospital. But the result had been a happy one, as were all her other births.

So we agreed to pay Karen Laing the $225 a month for prenatal care. She would perform the birth in the penthouse above the restaurant. The baby would not be born in a hospital. Elene was delighted, and we were reassured that at least a doctor was readily available.

The call came to Shirley the afternoon of March 5, 1982. Elene said her water had broken and she expected the baby to come soon. Karen was on her way. The soft lights and the background music were all ready. On the phone Shirley could hear violins and bassoons.

"What's the music?"

"'The Golden Voyage.' It's a lovely welcome into the world."

Shirley called me at my office. "The baby's coming, and I'm taking off now. I don't want you along." She was nervous, almost brutal. "You'll be in the way."

The afternoon Shirley left, the weather turned stormy with a violent March wind and rain. When she got to Santa Cruz the birth was over, the midwife gone, and Elene was already vacuuming. It was a boy and Elene had named him Gale. On this windy night the name made perfect sense.

The birth had gone smoothly. Elene used the squatting position over pads on the living room floor. "The Golden Voyage" ushered the newborn into a presumably harmonious world. I thought of it as a lovely delirium.

Shirley's first job on arrival was taking all the birth cloths, the bloody sheets and towels, to the laundromat. Alas, the apartment did not include a washer and dryer. In the days ahead she got to know that laundromat intimately. Her routine became laundromat, market, and kitchen.

Elene had carefully saved her placenta, which she intended to eat. It was a practice suggested by some midwives, borrowing from primitive habits and the animal world. Elene accepted the belief that it restored a mother's nutritional balance. Shirley in her nightly reports to me complained of facing that dish of afterbirth in the fridge every morning. "But she isn't eating it very fast."

Over the next two years we traveled often to Santa Cruz and I held Gale many times. Sight isn't the only sense needed to enjoy children. Just holding Gale, feeling him squirm or crawl over my shoulder, listening for the jabbers, presuming words, smelling his breath—these were the essence of pleasure; these were invitations to imagination.

Elene thrived on motherhood. She converted the living room into a child's room. She found in an alley an abandoned rack that she used to keep her many baby books flat and accessible. She hung a net from the ceiling for a baby swing. She read to Gale constantly and when she wasn't reading, she was playing music for him. I thought of Shirley's midnight Mozart for Elene.

Elene adapted and, whatever the strains, she was coping well. We breathed sighs of relief. It's highly possible that we weren't watching that closely, though, for my attention was coming to focus on Shirley. She was having trouble with her hips. They were stiffening rapidly and hurting her severely. She had already been forced to use a walker. The doctors had said it was not arthritis but a dying bone mass at the joints. It would not improve with medication, massage, or exercise. It required hip replacements. Fearfully we scheduled the first surgery for the third week in December and the second for early March.

While wrestling with these problems, we had a call from Santa Cruz. After Elene asked about Shirley, she sheepishly said, "I have some news for you." Her tone was such that I feared immediately what she had to say, and I think Shirley did, too. "I'm pregnant again."

I was glad I was sitting. I felt weak all over. I think my first thought was of Gale, barely two. Is that timing good or bad? Considering Elene's particular problems, was time on her side or against her?

Shirley and I started a whole new set of nighttime worries, talking for hours in bed before sleep. Would two babies impossibly multiply the strain? Or did the way she had taken to motherhood suggest that children were good therapy for her? For Shirley it was wrenching that she would not be able to help, for the new baby was due in March. "You know where I'll be then."

In early December Shirley's first surgery went well.

Elene was not unmindful of Shirley's trauma. That Christmas she bought a Unicef card. It had the picture of a little girl dragging a tree across a snowy field. She wrote this message on it:

Dear Mom,

    I intended to get this to you in the hospital. I thought maybe the picture was how you got Christmas trees as a little girl. I'm so glad your surgery turned out so well. I wish I could be more of a help to you and not always in need of your help.

Love,

Elene

A lovely card! But we did not receive it that Christmas, but rather in February of 1987, three years later. At the bottom of the card Elene penned an addendum: "Mom, Here's a Christmas card I never got off to you from a couple of years ago."

Three years late! There was that time-warp again. Did these lapses ever bother her? Probably not. Take things as they come. Never let the uneven places wear you down. For Elene a rigid attachment to time was an unnecessary restraint in a world so full of hazard.

When Elene was some eight-and-a-half months along, she was riding the bus on her way to Karen's office for a regular check-up. The bus was between stops on Soquel Avenue when Elene felt her water break.

"Driver," she called, "I'm having a baby." She exhibited no panic. She was telling the driver a simple statement of fact.

The driver turned and saw her soaked dress. Seeing she wasn't kidding, he stopped the bus at the next corner and came back to her.

"You're having a baby?" There was panic in his voice, if not in hers.

"Yes. Karen Laing's office is at Soquel and 41st. That's where I'm heading."

The driver said he couldn't handle this. She had to get off.

So Elene got off, clutching herself, but not overly concerned. She went into the nearest shop. The woman there could see the need and called a taxi, which came in quick time. It got her to Karen's office, pronto. Labor was well under way.

Karen swung into action. She had a special room. Soft music was turned on. (This time was it "A Silver Voyage"?)

Karma was called and he brought Gale. They barely got there when the baby came. It was an easy birth, no sedatives or unusual equipment. All natural with the father and two-year-old brother attending.

Elene sat in an easy chair for about an hour, holding the baby whom Karen had washed and blanketed. Then Elene said she was ready to go. She carried the new baby beside Karma and Gale, got in the car, and they started home. On the way she said she was hungry for Chinese food, so they stopped for some take-out, and then proceeded as if the four of them had been on a family outing.

It was March 15, 1984, and they named the baby Jonathan.

Alas, the subsequent time proved that coping with a second baby was not that simple. Within a couple of weeks Elene was on the phone crying inconsolably, moaning for all the things that weren't getting done. The house was a mess. The bathroom needed scrubbing. The dirty clothes were piled high. It was clearly more than postpartum blues, though that may have entered the picture.

We sought a series of college women to come in, clean, and baby-sit, but none lasted more than a week because they did not do things the way Elene wanted. One was too slow when they walked the babies. One smoked, and her breath carried toxic fumes. One wanted to use Lysol and Ajax, deadly chemicals for Elene.

Elene was an unusual mother. She considered breast feeding important for as long as possible, and Gale wasn't weaned 'til he was over two. When it came time for solid food, Elene chewed it herself before putting it in the baby's mouth. She allowed the boys to run naked in the house all morning, bouncing in the netted swing or nestling naked in the warm sand on the beach. When they were dressed it was only in natural fibers, cotton and wool, never polyester. Their toys were chosen for simplicity of materials like wood or wool. I knew Elene grieved deeply when later on the boys expressed interest in plastic toy weapons. Television for Elene was an absolute no-no. She mistrusted it as a deterrent to the development of children's minds and for years would not allow a set where the boys would be tempted by its seductions.

Their diet was probably ideal, avoiding all preservatives, steaming or broiling, never frying, lots of fresh fruit and vegetables and brown rice, organic if possible. She took pains to build their bodies strong and agile. She took Gale to a swim club for lessons his first summer and again the following spring when he was a year old. She enrolled both boys in Gymboree after they were two. Their balance was unusually good, and when we walked along sidewalks, they tended to jump from curb to curb and wall to wall. Their minds were being nourished. She used the public library and checked out books by the handful. We once counted twenty on her racks. And she considered nursery school important, found a fine one connected to Cabrillo College, and herself enrolled in a dance class to make Gale eligible.

In spring 1987 Shirley and I were walking with Elene and the boys down the Garden Mall one day on our way to a restaurant for lunch. We had our things packed in the car and were going to start our drive south right after lunch. The boys were five and three and Elene carried Jonathan on her back in a pack.

Gale had stopped and was down on the sidewalk where ants were forming a hill for a nest. "Isn't that beautiful?" Elene said to Gale. "Let's watch."

Shirley and I went ahead and sat on a bench waiting. The three of them must have spent ten minutes hunched over the anthill. They followed the line of ants to where they were finding sand for their hill. They watched ants helping one another. They saw a dead ant being carried back to the nest. I was getting antsy myself. We had intended to get to the restaurant before the noon rush so we could eat fairly quickly and get on the road. We hoped for Buellton before dark.

"God, will she ever come?" I muttered to Shirley.

She sighed and raised her eyebrows. "Not as long as those boys are interested in the ants. Obviously their education comes first."

In the next half block a liquid amber tree was shedding its leaves, and another session followed collecting leaves, comparing them, and carefully pocketing them.

We left them that day after lunch with Gale and Elene down on the pavement watching a crawling bug. "Well," said Shirley, "Spock says you can't really spoil a child."

Shirley and I settled into a pattern of visiting Santa Cruz four or five times a year—once for the boys' birthdays in March, again in spring or early summer, then in late summer or fall to buy clothes for school, and once again just before Christmas. These were the milestones in our lives. In the winter when it was stormy, we flew to San Jose and rented a car. In the nicer weather we drove (i.e., Shirley drove). In Santa Cruz we stayed in motels, for Elene's house never afforded an extra bed. Often we had the boys stay with us overnight at the motel, and they seemed to enjoy it, especially the swimming pool.

When the boys were still very young, they moved from their penthouse to the first floor of a Victorian house on Elm Street, still very close to the Garden Mall. On Elm Street we never expected to find a calm household. Outsiders trooped through the place. We got to know Tamarack, who was often at their house when he wasn't in his trailer in a vacant lot where he grew vegetables. Dasram came in to take his showers. I wondered how much they affected Elene's feelings.

In spite of her happiness with the babies, as the years went by Elene gradually succumbed to the strain. Her emotional stability deteriorated. She flew off the handle so quickly. We often felt we were walking on eggs when talking with her.

Once we were getting ready to go back south and were taking a few pictures of the boys. We were inside and so the flash came on automatically. Elene came into the room and started screaming at the top of her lungs. Through her screams she was saying the flashes had damaged the boys' eyes forever. We repeatedly reassured her that the blind spots were only temporary reactions.

Our talking seemed to make it worse. She wouldn't stop screaming, whatever we did. We decided to quickly kiss them all goodbye and get out as fast as possible. We could still hear her screaming as we drove off.

I felt awful. Were we cowards? Was it the right thing to leave? Should we have called the hospital? But wasn't that Karma's responsibility? And if we were the problem, maybe she quieted down after we left with our infamous camera.

We had always suspected that stress intensified the danger. We reasoned that part of the present strain must have been watching Karma's business going galley-west. He was selling health foods and vitamin supplements and the sales at first did fairly well. He overexpanded, even hiring subagents around the Bay area. But he was not good at hounding them to keep up their payments. Another company moved in and undercut prices. His sales plummeted.

I was beginning to repent my urging of the marriage. Sure, it had produced two wonderful boys, but the marriage itself wasn't providing a stable backdrop for them. Maybe Shirley had been right.

And there were other strains. There was a fundamental incongruity between Elene and Karma. For example, his smoking. She hated smoking and believed all the emerging reports of its ill effects on the smoker as well as those nearby. When the babies came, the feelings intensified. For a while she got him to smoke outside, but that didn't last.

They disagreed on television. And they disagreed on birth control. For Shirley and me, who had faced birth control so carefully, the disagreement between Elene and Karma on that question was far more important than smoking or TV. Karma claimed their second child was an "accident" caused by Elene's belief that birth control was a form of killing. He blamed it on her, but at the same time he would not think of a vasectomy. We suspected their answer was abstinence and, as far as we could tell, they had stopped having sex.

Their disagreements hit me hardest when they came to violence. Elene cried on the phone one night that Karma had hit her in the head.

I called him immediately. "Yes," he said. "I hit her, but she hit me even harder."

I was furious. They sounded like kindergarteners.

"She was screaming," he went on. "It's the only way I know to stop her."

My mind tangled. "That's no kind of therapy," I shouted. "There's no excuse for hitting your wife. Don't you realize you could seriously hurt her? She's the mother of your children. How would you like it if she was seriously injured? What would you do then?" My voice was rasping and harsh. It got louder. "Don't you claim to love her? Don't you claim to respect her?" At that point if he had been in front of me and I could have seen what I was doing, I would have tried to strangle him.

He didn't say anything, only made a low "uh-huh" kind of sound.

I was just getting wound up. "Have you thought what it means to the boys? This world may be a violent world, but you can at least try to make it better, and giving those boys the model of violence is the worst possible lesson. Violent fathers create violent children. Where's your Oriental religion? Don't you believe in nonviolence?"

Again I got a low "Uh-huh."

I was beginning to calm down. "Love is precious and tender. It can't stand blows. Life is hard enough as it is." He made another "Uh-huh," and I said, "We'll talk again," and hung up.

Through it all Elene still claimed that she loved him. She said it many times, and I'm sure she meant it.

Then she told us that she had thrown her wedding ring down the toilet.

A wedding ring down a toilet? The ring from the man she loved? Toilets are a long way from expressing love. Sleepless, hearing Shirley breathe heavily beside me, love suddenly seemed strange to me. I guess sometimes it can mean only sex and sometimes, maybe often or always, it can mean pain. It seemed so different with Shirley and me, but then Elene and Karma weren't Shirley and me. Is love something different to each of us? Maybe Elene had given up on finding too much in love. On the other hand, when the ring was gone she still said she loved him. He was her man. She had chosen him. He had chosen her. Their sex had given them jewels of sons. So why shouldn't she say she loved him still, rational or otherwise, even after the ring was down the drain?

But, as usual, I was probably wrestling too much with events. Should I assume that Elene's mind was playing its sad tricks and let it go at that? Slipping in and out of mental illness has to result in actions that are simply unaccountable. Trying to understand them is a bit like asking if dreams have meaning. Since I believe they do, perhaps I can be forgiven for attaching meaning to a ring down a toilet in Elene's life.

Chapter Nine

Second Sight

To be honest, though, these were days in which Elene's marriage was not front and center in our minds. Whatever the marriage foreboded, Shirley and I had stumbled onto a heavenly miracle.

I had reconciled myself to blindness. The doctors had ruled out surgery. By the late 1970s my vision was virtually gone. I could detect hand movement at three feet in the good eye. I used a white cane. I had a talking computer. I had learned Braille, even Grade Three, the shorthand version. Though I continued to lecture and write, I hated the burden I was putting on others—friends, the history department, students, and especially Shirley. I blessed Shirley every time I prayed, and together we were coping pretty well. I was prepared for blindness the rest of my life.

Then in the mid-1980s my eyes began bothering me in unusual ways. They felt grainy and irritated. I reported to my ophthalmologist at Kaiser, Dr. Jeanne Killeen, who had shepherded me through the years. Many times she had patiently explained to me that the mature, dense cataracts that caused my blindness were inoperable due to the underlying uveitis. She had sent me to several distinguished ophthalmologists in Los Angeles for second opinions, and they had all agreed that surgery would be a mistake. Now she did some tests, found a sudden, alarming rise in pressure, and said we were in another ballpark.

"Surgery has become essential," she said. "The cataracts are leaking and causing glaucoma. We have to operate, whatever the risks. The alternative is severe pain, perhaps the loss of the eyeball. The surgery will avoid that. What your eyes will be like without the cataracts is anyone's guess. Your retinas have been hidden from us for a long time." She assumed, however, that the years of inflammation had destroyed the possibility of much vision. She scheduled emergency surgery for Tuesday, March 25, 1986.

On Wednesday, the day after the surgery, the bandages were removed, and, miracle of miracles, the eye had stubbornly defied the negative predictions. I saw my Shirley's face for the first time in fifteen years. I counted the stripes on her blouse and their yellows and blues and greens made my heart jump. It was speech, not vision, that I lacked now.

Shirley drove me home. I rode in a daze. Colors crowded in from everywhere—the cars, the landscaping, the signs, the Mondrian stripes on the streets. We drove into our garage and I could see the dirty rags and the piles of boxes—everything was beautiful. I could see our condominium for the first time. A new world had been born. You can imagine the excitement of the next weeks as the vision in my right eye improved and sharpened and then settled at 20:40.

We drove to Santa Cruz early that spring. When we walked into the Elm Street house, the boys greeted us, saying their mom was in the bathroom. We could hear her voice faintly. "I'll be right there."

Gale and Jonathan—there they were, not the way I had imagined them, but simply wonderful. At two and four their faces were not the baby faces I had thought; they were longer, surrounded by halos of hair. I had to sit down. I don't think they realized what was going on in my mind, but I had to sit down. Shirley went off looking for Elene. The boys brought me a book. I read them *Green Eggs and Ham*. The eggs were bright green and the ham was glorious red, but the real gems—precious rubies for sure—were the smiling faces of the boys. I'm sure they had no idea why I hugged them after each chapter.

Soon Elene came in followed by Shirley. I stared at Elene. I had not seen her clearly since she was fifteen years old. Standing before me was a grown, well-developed woman with long, soft brown hair that fell around her shoulders, a broad forehead and well-shaped chin, and hazel eyes that expressed joy. I no longer saw a teenager, but a strikingly good-looking woman in the prime of her life.

There were so many features of Elene that seemed new to me—her body contours, the maturity of her face, even a few lines around her eyes, but she was still my Elene. There were those kind eyes, the bright eyes of intelligence and eloquence. Her smile had not changed. If anything, it was more beautiful, especially when she was looking at her boys.

When I smiled at Elene, I wondered if she could now look into my one clear eye in ways she had wanted to when she was young. Was I a new person for her? If she had two personae, one when she was ill and quite another when she was well, was I in the same way now someone else? How much mutation comes with new sight? Will our relationship change? Was it too late for me to be the normal father? Was her normal childhood wish to have the most handsome, strongest father in the world completely washed away by years of realism? Our past may have been unreachable, but our future was structured with a hundred branched paths.

"We'll come back to Seuss later," she said. "Let's go to dinner now." She looked at me and whispered, "I am so happy."

The months ahead for me were jumbles of emotion. Most of the time I was agog at my new sight, and the faces of Shirley, Elene, and her boys were top on my list of delights. But one emotion bothered me deeply. There were times when I wasn't sure I was happy with the new situation. During my blind years, so much had been done for me, so much had been granted me because of my blindness, so many allowances made, that I couldn't help worrying whether I would measure up when I was sighted like everyone else. I understood what was meant by postoperative depression. Sometimes I'm sure it was just overload. Some of it was the hard job of organizing sense impressions once more. Much of it was disappointment in finding the seen not as exciting as the imagined. But much, too, was the absence now of the halo of admiration, a felt loss of security that blindness provided. This is the point when many people whose vision is restored after long blindness seek a return to blindness and the refuge it provided.

Then it hit me that my experience may not have been that different from Elene's. For me there was a kind of torment that occurred when sight was regained. Was there a vaguely similar torment for Elene when rationality was regained? A refuge was removed. That special security that was a buffer from the real world was taken away. And if these feelings emerged, might they help explain the reversion to illness that so often came about? I never mentioned this to Elene. There are times when I think the idea is preposterous, but I cannot escape the possibility.

Chapter Ten

Hello Darkness, My Old Friend

We decided to buy a new car and give our old, comparatively reliable green Buick to Elene. We reasoned it would help her with the boys, especially since Karma's Dodge seemed always broken down. Elene was happy at the thought. She had had Driver's Ed in high school, took a refresher course, and got her license. We drove the car up, planning to fly back.

Elene took to the car right away, and I drove with her a few times while she bucked and jerked, then smoothed out. Thereafter she was a careful driver. She always made the boys sit in the backseat and buckle up. As I watched her driving and imagined how it would simplify her life, I thought we had made a good move.

We were sitting in the Elm Street house, weary from a morning of shopping with Gale and Jonathan at the Capitola Mall. The boys were five and seven. It was early fall, and we had come up for the fall outfitting. They loved our shopping sprees, but the occasions were fun for us, too, especially for me with my new sight.

We had trudged through Mervyn's, and JCPenney, and countless shoe stores, trying to keep up, always enjoying their excitement. Back at the house Shirley and I were bushed, but Jonathan was flying around on the net swing doing some kind of somersaults. The house was cool and we had slipped off our shoes and were stretching our toes when Elene came in with a man. We had seen him before as one of the people who drifted in and out of their house but we had never met him. He was a hulk with flowing beard, wild curly hair, and glasses. He wore a cape that looked like a former blanket stitched with a cord on one side. His pants were loose and also tied with a hemp string. He wore rope sandals. He was a big man, probably six feet and rounded out. He seemed quite at home.

He introduced himself as Oracle Abo.

"Do you room here?" I asked.

"I live in my trailer down the block, but I pay skinflint Karma to use his bathroom."

Elene must have thought she was helping by adding, "Oracle grows vegetables. He brings some to us."

Carrots, not cash, I thought.

I went ahead with my probing. "Where do you work?"

"I'm a healer. I'm a messenger from the new age." He pulled from his pocket a wrinkled brochure with a picture of Oracle on the cover with his hand uplifted as if he were Jesus in blessing. Inside were testimonials of healing, and in a quick glance I noticed that Karma Carlson claimed to have been cured of his tired feeling.

"You can read my testimonials," Oracle said. Then he changed to a confidential tone. "I'm about to close a deal on some land in Palm Springs. I have a partner who lives in Beverly Hills."

"Great," I said, but I certainly didn't think this malarkey was great.

He sat down next to me. The new age didn't exactly smell like roses. He leaned close. "You're Elene's father, right?" I nodded, edging away slightly. "You ought to do something about Karma."

"What's the problem?"

"He treats her like shit." The new age used rather earthy language.

That night we took them all out for dinner. Karma said very little and was notably cool to Oracle. In fact, we noticed that Elene sat beside Oracle with the boys on the other side of her. Karma was beside Shirley.

The next morning we arrived about nine thirty thinking we'd take Elene for some fall clothes. The boys were still asleep and so was Karma.

"I don't want any clothes," she said, before we had even sat down. And then, as if it were no more than the color of a dress, she dropped a bomb in our laps. "But you should know that I'm pregnant."

I sat down and looked at my lap. Elene pregnant again! I felt vaguely dizzy, but I made a brave smile and came out with, "Is Karma happy?"

"He's not the father."

I was getting less dizzy and more upset. "Who's the father?"

"Oracle."

Shirley was taking it in stride. "Look, Elene, we should talk about terminating the pregnancy."

Elene looked at Shirley as if there were shards of ice projecting from her eyes. She turned abruptly, started moaning, and left by the front door, slamming it behind her so hard I was sure the pane of glass had cracked.

Shirley just looked at me and shook her head. "Oh, Robert," she whispered, and was almost crying. I held her close. We sat in that quiet house with Elene gone and the others asleep for half an hour, holding one another. We felt like sailors in a cabin with pounding seas outside and a sense of certain shipwreck ahead.

Back in Riverside we buckled down and decided our role was to be as helpful as we could. We hired Karen Laing again. At least we could see Elene to a healthy birth. We weren't brave enough to go up for the birth itself, rationalizing it was better for them that way.

But we heard the whole story. The baby was born in August at home on Elm Street and was named Micah. We never knew whether the name came from the Bible or from thin, tough minerals. We called the night of the day Micah was born. The picture was as expected: Elene was already cooking supper for them all.

In place of going up we sat at home and fumed, but we concluded that our presence in Santa Cruz would be like grains of sand in the eye. We were not the ones to help in this situation. I imagined Oracle taking no responsibility, probably soon disappearing. He didn't have any money anyway. Certainly Elene shouldn't exchange Karma for him, and our pushing against it might foster the opposite. It was possible that she and Karma would work it out. We concluded that the best we could do was stand by as distant support. For a time anyway, the telephone would be our bridge—Simon and Garfunkel's bridge over troubled waters.

Three weeks later in Riverside, sound asleep at three thirty in the morning, we gradually wakened to knocking. I stumbled to the front door and found Elene, baby Micah in arms, Gale and Jonathan in the dark behind her.

"Elene! How did you get here?"

Shirley was up by now and we helped them in. "Drove. We didn't know it would take so long."

"It's seven or eight hours," I said, still amazed.

"We didn't leave 'til afternoon. We found a beautiful lake."

Shirley took the baby while they all went to the bathroom.

"The baby needs changing," Shirley called.

All we heard from the bathroom was, "I forgot to bring diapers," as if that took care of the matter.

Shirley mumbled as she sorted some hand towels for diapers. In the kitchen she got out milk and cookies and apples. Meanwhile I rounded up as many mats and blankets as I could find. Our little second bedroom had only a single bed in it. The boys would have to sleep on the floor. When they bedded down, Elene too took the floor, so no one ended up in the bed.

Shirley and I didn't sleep much the rest of the night. We were up by six thirty, having coffee and muffins when Elene came in to nurse Micah.

Shirley said, "I'll get some disposable diapers at the market first thing."

"No. No. They've got chemicals in them. I don't use them."

"Towels don't work very well and I've not got enough of them."

"The stores have cloth diapers."

"I'm not so sure anymore."

"They do in Santa Cruz."

"Santa Cruz is another world."

My mind was working in other directions. "Whatever got into you to come down without telling us?"

"We just wanted to come. Karma said we should come."

"Karma put you out?"

"He said we should try it apart for awhile. He said he might want a divorce."

Hello, darkness, my old friend. So she's pushed into the arms of Oracle. I felt sick to my stomach. I shoved the crumbling muffin away and drank coffee.

"I'm going over to Loretta's for a minute." Shirley got up and left.

It suddenly occurred to me that we had been terribly negative since Elene had come. I changed tones. "It's awfully good to see you. This will be our first visit with Micah."

Elene smiled, I think for the first time since she had come.

I went on, "Just might be the bravest thing I've heard in ages, setting out alone with a baby and two little boys."

"Gale and Jonathan slept most of the way."

"But you had the baby, too."

"He was in the front seat with me. I pulled off and nursed him when he cried."

She turned sad. "Oh, Papa, I think they want to take him away from me."

"Who?"

"Someone has reported me to the children's people. They've called."

Shirley came back with arms loaded. "Look. Loretta had piles of diapers that she's no longer using. And she sent some clothes for Micah, too. Her boys have outgrown them." The little shirts, pants, and sweaters looked almost new.

Shirley held up a light blue sweater.

Elene studied the label. "It's acrylic," she said, as if it were radioactive. "I want him to wear cotton or wool."

We had a picnic in the park that noon. Shirley and I thought we had a good time, but that night Elene told us we moved too slowly. "I can't live with you," she said. "You move so slow."

I thought, That's no news. Didn't we already know that?

Elene seemed edgy, we assumed because Karma had put her out.

On the fourth day Elene announced that she could stand it no longer and had to get back to Santa Cruz. "I need more spontaneity," she said. "Santa Cruz has more spontaneity."

I thought she sure hit that nail on the head. I said, "How will you get back?"

"Same way I got down here."

"Shirley or I will drive with you. I could take care of the kids. Shirley could help you drive."

She made a strange moaning sound and said, "No. No. No."

I heard her on the phone to Karma. She was pleading. From the other room it sounded as if she were crying. I think she was saying, "I can't stay here. I can't."

When she came back, she said, "Karma says I can move back. I'll go tonight. The boys and the baby will sleep."

Pure nightmare! Should we let her do it? Could we stop her? Driving three children, one a baby, all night, was sheer madness. I even considered calling the mental health people. But I knew they wouldn't listen. She was not being the required threat to others or to herself. Hah, I thought, she was certainly being a threat to others and herself. Still I knew they would not see it that way. I had talked with enough of them to know that.

In the end I bent and bowed. Feeling no longer in control, I had to turn to trusting instincts. Now I had to trust Elene's. If she could make it down, she could make it back. What else could I do? I had her car checked, lubed, and filled with gas. Shirley was as upset as I was, but she spent the day making sandwiches and buying bags of oranges and apples, bottles of fruit juice, and raw vegetables, which she cleaned and sliced. I stuffed some cash in Elene's wallet. All the time we lashed in our minds to think how we could prevent this horror.

Anything we said provoked in Elene wild reactions. I thought she was near the breaking point. If she were going to break down, it was better that she be in Santa Cruz. They knew her there. She knew them. And I whipped myself again for being heartless. Was I simply throwing the burden on someone else? But I was helpless anyway. Heartless and helpless. Helpless again.

That was the last time we saw Micah. When we hugged and kissed goodbye and they drove off in the dark, I turned to Shirley. "No parents in their right minds would let them do that."

Shirley shrugged. "They made it down. They'll make it back."

The next day the worries rose notch by notch. Leaving at eight, they should have gotten to Santa Cruz by six in the morning, even allowing a couple of hours for stops.

We called Karma at nine. Not there. No word. We called at ten. We called at twelve. Not there. No word.

We called the state highway patrol to check on accidents. None reported on the coast highway during those hours. That was a minor relief. It was too early to report them missing. Where were they? Had they been held up? Were they lost? By night our minds had woven terrible tapestries of danger and catastrophe. And the basic warp was our own guilt at having let them do it.

At ten that night we jumped when the phone rang. It was Gale's high-pitched voice.

"Hello, Grandpa."

"Gale, where are you?"

"Home."

"Where have you been?"

"We saw sharks in the aquarium. We saw their teeth."

"Let me talk to your mother."

Elene admitted they had made quite a few stops. "We looked for the Venice canals. I've always wanted to see them. But we never found them. It was too dark. When it was getting dawn, I was tired and we went off to a lake somewhere above Santa Barbara. The sun rose over silver water."

Tears were in my eyes. I could only think of *Sail on, silver girl, sail on by*.

Elene was continuing. "We ate breakfast on the grass. We went to a Christmas tree farm. The trees had dew all over them. We went out to a beach somewhere and cows were watching us. We picked up a hitchhiker on his way to the Big Sur Jazz Festival."

Oh, my dear God, a hitchhiker with three little kids in the car.

"He was so nice. He drove while I nursed the baby."

Oh, God, are you really in your Heaven?

"To get him to his festival, we had to go by way of Monterey, so we went to the aquarium. We couldn't find my wallet. I wondered if maybe the hitcher had taken it, but we searched and found it behind the seat. We shouldn't have worried."

I thought of guardian angels shepherding those four home, to put it mildly. And we worried still. There was something bizarre about the whole thing: the lack of preparation for the trip when she drove down, the obliviousness to danger, the lack of concern for the children. I said to Shirley, "I wonder if it's a call for help from Elene. Karma is threatening. She finds she can't live with us. So why not pick up hitchhikers and detour to the aquarium?"

And then another of those dreaded calls came. It was the Santa Cruz police. From them and others we pieced together the story. Elene had gone out—this was a cold February day—to walk on the Pacific Garden Mall. I imagined the sycamore leaves piled in the gutters and picked up by the boys searching for color. The boys were dressed all right, but Micah was naked. There were lots of people on the mall. One woman notified a policeman that Elene was endangering a child by exposing him naked in public on a cold day. To the policeman, Elene must have acted strangely, at least from his standpoint. He took her to jail where she stayed four days for child endangerment. We learned that story only after the fact.

The jail seemed to bother Elene little, but the fact that Micah was at the same time placed in foster care drove her up the wall. She was released from jail on the condition that she be psychologically tested by the Children's Protective Agency.

Two weeks later she was reunited with Micah. On the phone to us she lamented, "They have severed the bond. It can never be the same."

After a few sobs, she went on. "I feel things happening, though. My instinctive response is heightened. I am beginning to respond to other things than just Micah. How can I care for Micah now that the bond is severed?"

"Is that a problem?" I asked.

"I find myself feeling I have to go somewhere and do something. Yesterday I had to walk two blocks in one direction and I had no choice. I had to do something, but I couldn't find out what it was. It was terrible. Whenever I get there something terrible happens. The police arrive or a fire breaks out. I need someone to care for Micah four hours a day. That's all. Four hours a day."

These were weeks in which psychiatrists and psychologists were interviewing and testing Elene. Dr. Gordon Peretz, a clinical psychologist, wrote the final report for the court. He sent a copy to us. He recommended:

1) Foster care for Micah for six months followed by re-evaluation. If little progress, then adoption.
2) Parenting and couples' therapy groups for Elene and Karma.
3) Child care and other support from county agencies.
4) Greater help from grandparents.

Number four slammed into us, but number one hit Elene the hardest. For days Elene was on the phone every day, mostly in tears. She was crushed by the report. She called it cruel. She feared losing Gale and Jonathan as well as Micah. She once even said she wanted to take the boys and leave Karma. She wanted to find some kind of cooperative community where the group helped raise the children. She wanted some live-in help. She wanted Micah back. She was distraught.

Then she began to quote Karma all the time. He claimed the solution to all their problems would be a house of their own. We should buy it and they would rent it from us. He said the owners of the Elm Street house were making noises about wanting them out. Security from such threats would make a big difference for them.

Shirley thought the house idea was a good one. Maybe it would be an answer to that fourth directive on the Peretz report, the one about grandparents. This was a way to help. We could afford it. And if they broke up, we could always sell the house.

I reluctantly came to agree. Karma and Elene were already looking around. They found a shack with a tarpaper roof and ten acres of land in Davenport, fifteen miles north of Santa Cruz, at an exorbitant price. We vetoed that.

We called Santa Cruz agents. One offering was a house with two bedrooms and a den, a full kitchen, and modern bath in Ben Lomond, a reasonable location in the San Lorenzo Valley just above Santa Cruz. Everything we asked and everything the agents said sounded right to us. We made an offer, contingent on our coming up the next day to inspect. We left at 4:00 A.M., picked up Elene and Karma about eight thirty, and reported to the agent. Alas, the house had been sold by another agent the night before to someone who offered a thousand dollars over the asking price.

We took off immediately to look at other places, but we couldn't agree on anything. By late afternoon we were all tired and at an impasse. We said we'd have to postpone the search 'til we could come up again, which we would try to do soon.

The period that followed was a hard one. We had interminable discussions about houses with agents and Karma, but Elene would not talk with us. Her mind seemed to interweave the problem of the house with her deepest fears of losing Micah and, even more so, losing the boys.

Later that month the social agents came with a court order and took Micah back to a foster home.

Karma called us with that news. "They just came one morning about eleven. They said they were sorry. They said maybe it would work out and Micah could come back."

"How did Elene react?"

"I saw tears in her eyes, but she didn't scream or anything. She kept repeating, 'You've broken the bond.'"

I fell into one of those funks where I couldn't tell how I felt. I could see those tears in Elene's eyes but I also knew that Shirley thought the adoption of Micah would be Elene's salvation. I wondered about salvation through suffering, and I realized I wasn't far from my Christian roots—suffering as a means of salvation. But hasn't Elene had enough?

After that we learned from Karma that Elene was often not at home. He was complaining that he had to care for the boys alone. Our thoughts were on Elene, wondering where she was.

With Elene missing, the house idea now seemed out of the question. Now our fears centered on whether Karma might divorce Elene, as he had threatened.

Karma continued to complain. He said Elene had let her driver's license expire. She was now staying away from home for days at a time. Karma said she was getting acupuncture. He told us she had spent time some weeks ago in the mental hospital. That disturbed us because we hadn't even known of it. But, he said, after she was discharged, she was still gone a lot.

When we went up in December to get the boys their Christmas things, Elene was missing. Karma had reported the fact to the police. I called them, too, and the police said they had her name and description on record, but there were so many missing people in Santa Cruz, most of them drifting with the homeless, that we should not be optimistic.

We tried to cover our feelings by busying with all the Christmas preparations, buying and wrapping presents, but always hoping that we would run into Elene. One night Karma said she had come home for a few hours in the night and left right away. We concluded she did not want to see us.

It was more than that. She had become a street person. In our motel every night we huddled and moaned out some version of *what can we do*? Karma had described one of the vans she was often seen in—sideboards on the bed of a pickup with a peaked plastic roof. He had seen it near Mark West Park. He said it looked like a fairytale gingerbread house on wheels, except as he described, "it was kind of moth-eaten." He didn't think Elene even knew the people she was living with.

When we had seen the kids to bed, Shirley and I drove to Mark West Park and wandered around like benign intruders into an unknown world. In subsequent days we got to know every park in Santa Cruz and there are lots of them—San Lorenzo, Laveage, Jade Street, Neary Lagoon, West Lake, Highlands, Nisene Marks. We saw plenty of unshirted men with hair long enough to shield their bodies and plenty of women in tattered mother hubbards or far less. A world of down-and-outers, rags on bones, torn packs on backs. We looked into countless faces, drove by endless small neighborhood parks where the homeless congregated, but we never found Elene.

We heard through a friend of Karma's that she had been seen with a man in a van parked near the Rio Theater.

My thoughts careened crazily. Camper shells and vans did provide a roof overhead and most likely food on some kind of table. All to the good. But the other Great Fear always crowded those thoughts out. She was living with people we didn't know, young men whom we had no reason to trust. Could they even trust themselves? And how many times had Shirley and I expressed our overriding fear—another pregnancy? I longed for the hospitalizations because they at least protected Elene from young men.

We drove round and round the Rio Theater. We parked on side streets for hours until we lamely joked that the police would take *us* in for suspicious loitering.

One night in a triangle park on Soquel not far from the Staff of Life market, we saw a woman whose shape from the car looked like Elene. Shirley and I got out and walked closer. My new eyesight looked into her face and it wasn't Elene. My heart swelled for this woman. She was obviously stoned, gliding in her own space, only half aware of us. I said, "Excuse me; we thought you were someone else."

She looked at me wearily. "You look like my dad."

I said, "I'll bet he'd like to see you."

She thought a minute. "Don't you believe it. Don't you believe it."

Those nights were like walking with Dante into the Inferno. Each park was a new circle of hell. The difference was that the inhabitants were only suffering from our point of view. I had read the *Teachings of Don Juan*. I suspected that, like him, these people were touched with fire, the fire of their drug world. Don Juan's fire was intense color, violent, outrageous color. I wondered what these people were seeing when they twanged their guitars and sang the song I remembered so well—"Hello darkness, my old friend"—that song of longing. How could they not be longing for all they had left? To us these ragged shapes were far from color. They were, indeed, in a terrible darkness—hello, darkness—and Elene was somewhere in there with them.

We needed no statistics to tell us that most of these people were mentally ill. They needed care. As we searched in the night, park after park, our thoughts often returned to the sixties and Governor Ronald Reagan and his dismantling of the entire state mental hospital system. We weren't so critical of the idea then because we hated the picture of human beings moldering in mental health wards, the snake pits of electric shocks and lobot-omies. We had assumed that the funds that went to state hospi-tals would be dispersed to local facilities for the care of the mentally ill. But, alas, the funds were used to buttress the budget, and the plan became a tax-saving device. So here, Ronald Reagan, were your wandering, sick, homeless children, and somewhere among them was our daughter.

One day we were walking with the boys down Water Street, headed from our motel to shop on the mall. We walked by other motels, and then we saw three figures—a woman and two men—approaching from the other end of the block. As we drew closer, it hit me like a hammer—it was Elene! Her hair was flowing down on all sides. She wore an Indian bedspread dress, the kind she liked, but this one looked grimy. Three strands of colored wooden beads were around her neck. The men had beads, too, metal ones, and earrings. Their hair was as long as Elene's. They were expression-less while Elene was smiling to see us. She hugged the boys.

"When are you coming home?" Gale said.

"I don't know. I'm making lists of what I need to do to straight-en things out. Ask your Dad."

I tried to hug her, and she accepted my hug for a moment but then pushed away.

"I don't want to do that," she said.

"Let us take you home," I said.

"Where? Why would I want to do that?"

"Because we love you," Shirley said. I thought I saw Shirley's eyes water.

"Don't worry about me. I'm fine."

"Are you sure?" I said. And Shirley was saying, "We want to take you home. You can come with us or you can go home with the boys. We'll talk with Karma."

Elene was visibly upset. "No," she said. "I won't do it."

One of the men said, "Elene lives with us."

"What's your name?"

"I'm Dave. This is Krishna." Krishna was grinning, but he seemed unable or unwilling to talk. Dave went on, "We're all fine. Don't get uptight."

My mind proposed that we take Elene by the arm and physically lead her with us. But I looked at those husky kids. They clearly wouldn't let us take her forcefully, even if we could, which I also knew we couldn't.

I could take her with the help of the police, but I doubted if I could get the police in time. And would the police be willing to intervene? She wasn't breaking any law or endangering herself. And, even if they would, where would that get us? She would violently resist. We would become her enemy. The boys would see her in the worst possible way. And she would end up in the hospital, where we knew she was headed no matter what we did.

They walked on smiling. Jonathan ran a bit after Elene, but Shirley caught him. He began to cry. I don't think Elene heard him. How could she and still walk on? No, she was in another world. Her mind was twisted on some cold path. I felt something move through me like a hard piece of ice that melted slowly into sorrow.

That isn't my Elene. That's a completely different person. Is this why older psychologists used to call schizophrenia a split personality? No, she wasn't split. She was one person split from reality. Or one person embracing a completely different reality. Her reality might be just as clear to her as mine is to me. Her world is real, too, isn't it? What if those wooden beads are emeralds to her? Then they're emeralds, not my kind of emeralds, but still emeralds.

But what an enormous gap between our realities! I can see no bridge.

She loves her boys. I know that. But she's thinking of that love in some different way. She's lost a link in expressing that love, like a lost button that she'll search for tonight under every piece of furniture. Will she wonder why David and Krishna look so little like Gale and Jonathan?

"Grandpa. Grandpa," Gale was repeating, finally jolting me back to what I called reality. "Can we get some honey ice cream on the way?" The reality of honey ice cream made sense to me. We got the biggest scoops possible.

We were scheduled to leave for Riverside the next day. Should we go? We had to get home. My classes were waiting.

Shirley had obligations. We had done what we could for the boys. We had failed miserably with Elene, but the failure was complete. Period. Hit the road. Give up again. Return to the reality of our Riverside world.

In the weeks that followed, our knowledge of Santa Cruz events suffered a time warp, always delayed, largely because we were not able to talk with Elene. When we learned of events from Karma or even from Gale, the incidents had usually happened the week before—always after the fact, always too late for us to do anything.

Once Karma told us Elene had been in the hospital for a week, not wanting us to know. She blocked the social workers from calling us. That time the hospital must have been a haven, for we heard she had been in jail three times, six days in all, for trespassing in the Santa Cruz Book Store. It was easy to picture. She was not a customer; she was a street person. Her compulsive talking must have bothered legitimate customers. I imagined the manager asking her to leave. I imagined her arguing endlessly with all kinds of strange explanations—maybe she was the one chosen to warn the store of toxic fumes from the smoke alarms—but not departing. After this pattern was repeated several times, the police took her to the hospital.

So she had been exiled from the bookstore. It made me sad because I knew how she loved that bookstore, that warm retreat from the technological world into shelves of books she had once loved or could love anew.

We called the doctor, Dr. James. He confirmed that while she was in the hospital she hadn't wanted us to know she was there, and he had respected her wishes on that score. He had placed her on Navane, Cogentin, and Lithium, and he was optimistic about the results.

We had often berated to ourselves the doctors who seemed so reluctant to diagnose, but we were coming to feel differently. We were reading Carol North's new book, *Welcome, Silence: My Triumph over Schizophrenia*. Her initial doctor had been merciless, immediately diagnosing schizophrenia and then assuming she could never get better and telling her boyfriend he would be wise to forget her, leave her to the mental professionals for life. We could be enormously grateful that no doctor had taken such an approach to Elene.

Not too long after that she phoned us. She called us collect, gave us the pay phone number, asked us to call the boys and call her back to tell her how they were. We considered that a good sign, but she broke down crying when she said Karma wouldn't let her come back to live there. She went on talking disjointedly and rambling without listening. She broke into a long wail. "They cut off my pubic hair."

"Who cut off your pubic hair?"

"Those men. They held me down."

"You mean Dave and Krishna?"

"No. A whole bunch of others."

How many times have I said that my mind boggled at the news? This time it was gyrating as it created this frightful picture— a bunch of young, bare armed, muscle-bulging men holding her down, laughing, spreading her legs, running an electric razor over her delicate parts, and then, and then—raping her? Oh, God, tell me it wasn't so. Tell me young men in that loving counterculture wouldn't act that way.

She was crying and I was speechless, but finally I said, "You're not pregnant are you?"

"No. I don't think so. I don't know what happened. But I know they cut off my hair."

"Had you taken drugs?"

"No. You know I don't take drugs."

"Could they have drugged you without your knowing?"

"I don't know, but I don't take drugs."

"You mean illicit drugs. I trust you're taking the doctor's prescriptions."

"I don't have any choice there." She was calming down.

She said, "When I'm on Navane, there're pulses through my brain, but every so often they slip, like little dams breaking."

What could I say about dams breaking in the brain? Chemical reactions, surely, but then the whole nature of her problems could be chemical reactions. I said, "I hope it's not too awful."

"No, not really. Little dams break everywhere in the world."

We talked a while about the boys. Then she said, "I think I'm going to SART next week."

"I always feel good when you're at SART. And after that, I know they have group houses you can stay in. You could see the boys often then."

We had a call from Dr. James. "I'm requesting a conservator-ship for Elene. I think she needs more help than another round at SART and then group housing. She needs those, too, but we also need to keep a closer eye on her, see that she takes her medica-tions and we have the right to prescribe for her. You'll be getting the legal papers. You may serve as her conservators, but we rec-ommend against that. We find in most cases parents don't work well in that role. A professional, outside eye is better all around."

This was a new question for us. We rummaged around for more information. We got books. E. Fuller Torrey, whose *Surviving Schizophrenia* was by now our bible, told us that studies showed conservatorships increased the percentage of stability in patients. We talked with the local conservators, the public defenders, the mental health people in Riverside.

It was a serious business in which Elene would be stripped of the right to vote and all freedom of contract. She could have no credit cards and make no legal agreements such as real estate transactions. She would always be provided legal counsel, howev-er, and the conservator would act on her behalf in such matters as divorce. The conservator would control her finances and parcel out her SSI. Elene would be assured of food, clothing, and shelter, but her public guardian could at any time assign her to the hospi-tal, a locked facility outside the hospital, or a board-and-care.

We talked with all the people involved in Santa Cruz and went up right away, making our usual Christmas visit a bit early. We talked with the man in social services who would act as her conservator.

He seemed right to us. He wore a ponytail. He was Santa Cruz laid-back. He was definitely the kind of person who could relate to Elene. We knew he would listen to her and be sympathetic. We signed the conservator papers.

With us back at home and Elene barely discharged from SART, Santa Cruz was devastated by an earthquake. The Loma Prieta quake leveled freeways all over the area, toppled buildings, scrambled brick fireplaces, started fires, and left hundreds homeless. The epicenter was in the Santa Cruz Mountains behind the city.

For a whole day we couldn't get through on the phone. Shirley and I took turns trying.

"Maybe they're all homeless now, Karma and the boys, too. If Elene is homeless again, this time she'll have more company."

Our newspapers were filled with pictures of broken Santa Cruz—the Cooper House on the mall a pile of rubble, likewise the Book Store building and Gottlieb's department store. We knew that mall like an old friend. It was a shambles, and the Elm Street house was just around the corner.

We finally got through to Elm Street. And who answered the phone but Elene.

"Are you all right?"

"We're fine, Papa. I was on the mall. It was beautiful. I saw great panes of glass bulging out. I stood there and exerted my will and I held them from breaking. They're still there. I can do that, Papa. They bulged out and I held them from breaking."

I said something vague like "I wish we could all do that," and then changed the subject. "How do you like your group house?"

"It's fine. Karma says I can come here during the day. He likes me to wash up the dishes and do the laundry."

"I should think so. You can be with the boys."

Our next trip up was an amalgam of joy in Elene's near recovery. We held the hope that the new public guardian arrangement could restructure her life, oversee finances, and provide care when needed, possibly even predict trouble and prevent it. We helped Elene fix up her room in the halfway house, buying a lamp she needed and a toaster oven. Karma still said she couldn't move back to Elm Street, but she spent her days there. That was their muddled version of a separation. Their family ship was sailing again, without sails, without keel, but afloat.

The couple who rented the upstairs of the Elm Street house were beginning to complain to the landlord. They said the boys made too much noise and that Karma and Elene screamed at each other. They were afraid the building would be set afire and they would be trapped upstairs. To Karma the landlord made the lame excuse that he needed their place for his ailing mother.

Karma was nervous. He had a friend who told him of a house available in Boulder Creek, ten miles up the San Lorenzo River beyond Ben Lomond. They could afford the rent, barely, especially since they expected a subsidy from Aid to Families with Dependent Children (AFDC). It was in the midst of an acre of redwoods, a magnificent grove for the boys to play in.

So they left the bustle of Elm Street and downtown Santa Cruz for the peace and solitude of Boulder Creek. Unfortunately in Elene's life it was the beginning of a hapless period of chaos.

My memories of Boulder Creek ricochet with images of drama, sadness, and despair alongside fun and laughter and the smell of redwoods. It was like fire itself—a flickering bearer of joys, sorrows, and pains. It was light repeatedly overcome by menacing shadows. Our lives—at least those of Shirley and me—were lit and warmed and burnt in Boulder Creek.

Chapter Eleven

Shards

The decision we made about that time was a big one: to move from Riverside after thirty-six years at the university, to pack up memories of our orange-grove house, of our later condominium, of Elene's arrival and childhood, of our weekends in Carlsbad, of Shirley's hip replacements, of my years of blindness, of my surprising second sight.

Shirley had faced the fact squarely that we needed to be in a retirement community where we could count on care and support for our remaining life. We looked at possibilities and chose one on the edge of another campus of the university in Irvine, California. Taking advantage of a good sellers' market, but moving far too fast for me, in three days we sold two homes—Riverside and Carlsbad—and our second car.

Then followed the agonizing disposal of belongings—pots and chairs in garage sales; lifetime treasures, silver and crystal, in estate sales; beds and shovels and the old Knabe piano to nieces and nephews who descended with pickups and trailers; books by the armloads to students and friends. Our adopted area, Orange County, was worlds apart in politics, climate, and culture.

Would our uprooting affect Elene? It did seem to us that following our move Elene deteriorated. Could the removal of a potential retreat have anything to do with that? She never said so, but is it possible that deep down she felt a refuge had been pulled from under her?

We did our best to compensate. We went up to Santa Cruz more often than usual. We maintained, even increased, our financial help. We tried to assure her that as long as we lived we would be at her side. The fact remained, however, that during these years there were long periods in which Elene grew hostile, accused us, hung up the phone, refused to talk with us, or disappeared completely.

We were in Santa Cruz for three days in March. We saw Elene only once. They were still in the Elm Street house waiting to move to Boulder Creek. We were in the living room helping the boys get dressed for an excursion on the mall. Suddenly Elene appeared at the outside door, and when we opened it, she stood there and started screaming, "I hate this society! I hate TV! I hate computers! I hate it! I hate it!"

I tried to hug her but she ran off down the street still talking wildly. I went out and could see her half a block away, pausing as if reconsidering, but when I tried to follow, she continued on. That helpless feeling sank to the pit of my stomach.

A few weeks later we heard from Karma that she had been seen in the River Street Homeless Shelter. We called there and left a message. "We love you and please call us."

We did get a call, but it was from Daly City, south of San Francisco.

"I'm not afraid of earthquakes," she said. "Will the boys be eating all right? Will you send them some money so they can eat right?"

"Yes, of course, but why are you in Daly City?"

"I don't need to tell you that."

"Why? We love you. We want to help."

"I'm fine. Just forget it." And she hung up.

We called the Daly City police and reported her missing. We gave them a detailed description. The policeman sighed and said, "Thank you for the information. We'll do what we can. But remember we have hundreds of missing young people and we can't pursue every one of them. They usually turn up."

Her next call was from Boulder Creek.

She said, "I can't stand it here. I want to live in a big city where there are museums and galleries and theaters. Here it's too quiet."

I tried to point out the advantages of Santa Cruz—people know you, you aren't rushing all the time, people use less technology. I thought the last would get to her.

"Oh, you never understand me." She sounded mad and hung up.

The next thing we knew she was in the Santa Cruz hospital. Karma told us the story. She had been out walking with the boys. She was on one side of the busy Boulder Creek highway and the boys were on the other. She was examining some rocks and the boys were watching a large spider. Someone had reported to the police that she was not protecting her children. The police took her to the hospital. They were getting to know her, we gathered, and in a strange sort of way, that was comforting to us.

Her talk from the hospital was steady and compulsive. We could not get a word in. She said she liked the homeless people of San Francisco and Daly City, but beyond that she didn't make a great deal of sense, interjecting comments about earthquakes and glass. Many times she reverted to the men holding her down and shaving off her pubic hair. "I'm not the same since."

We drove up to Santa Cruz and had a long talk with Dr. Calvin, who was trim, in his forties, but with an impressive beard, looking as if he would rather be at the beach. His office in the mental health unit was covered with potted plants—spider ferns, maidenhair ferns—none artificial. He had Elene's file on his desk. It was at least an inch thick. We knew that Dr. Calvin had been following Elene for at least two years. We had talked with him on the phone.

After the amenities, I confessed, "Lately I begin to feel disconnected with Elene. She often doesn't want to see us or talk to us. Should we let her go? She's a grown woman with a family. Maybe she'd do better without our interference."

"I know your feelings. And without admitting it even to yourselves, you're probably also thinking you would do better without her. Parents often take that stance, just go their own way. But how strongly can I say that's wrong? Your support is vital. She needs you whether she knows it or not."

"But what's the diagnosis? What's the prognosis? Surely you work on some diagnosis."

With a smile and a glint in his eye, he said, "I know you wouldn't want me to conclude anything from the fact that her birth date fits that widely proved fact that a high percentage of schizophrenics are born in the winter and spring months." Then he changed his demeanor. "But seriously, if you look through Elene's file you'll find manic-depressive, schizoaffective, occasionally full-fledged schizophrenia. Psychiatric diagnosis is never easy."

"Manic-depressive doesn't sound right to me," I offered. "She's manic often enough, but not followed by depression."

"I'm inclined to agree with you. That was an earlier doctor."

"So it's schizophrenia?"

"Possibly. We do find disordered thinking, disordered perception, disordered emotion, and those are all part of the illness. But I don't find the hallucinations associated with schizophrenia."

We had heard that before. At least the doctors seemed consistent. "Isn't holding back a plate-glass window an hallucination?"

"She's told me that story. It is a delusion, not a full-scale hallucination. She has many delusions, like her fear of microwaves and smoke alarms. But as you probably know, her delusions are often based on reasonable premises. She's a highly intelligent young woman. Still, delusions are not hallucinations."

Shirley said, "You're playing with words."

"What else can we play with?"

I was increasingly unhappy with this conversation. "I think we've known Elene to have hallucinations. After my mother died, she saw her grandmother come to her through a crack in the ceiling."

"I've not heard her say anything like that recently. That sounds like a real hallucination. But if you want a description of an extended hallucination, look at Joanne Greenberg's *I Never Promised You a Rose Garden*. That young woman has created a whole world, the world of Yr, and she uses it as her refuge. For Elene, it's possible her craving for the nontechnological world has become a hallucination for her, her world of Yr, her refuge. It's possible."

"But how do you determine treatment?"

"We treat her as if she had schizophrenia. She responds to psychotic drugs. She's on Navane now with Cogentin and Benadryl for side effects. We had her on Trilafon for a while, but the side effects were not good. Fortunately there're far better drugs in the pipeline."

"I trust you'll keep Elene in mind when they come along."

"Indeed so."

Soon afterward Elene was reassigned to SART and at first seemed to be doing fine there, even earning passes to take classes in sewing and fabrics at Cabrillo College. But after she was released, it was not long before she was back in the hospital. Released again, a month or so later, we had a collect call from her. She was in the Alameda Homeless Shelter across the bay from San Francisco. She had gone from Santa Cruz to Berkeley with followers of the Rainbow Tribe and then had wandered down to Alameda to find the shelter. Karma wouldn't let her come back to Boulder Creek, she told us as she cried. We wired her money for the bus back to Santa Cruz, then drove up ourselves to find her living with a Yogi named Satyananda. We pleaded with her to come back home with us, but she said no, she would scream all the way if we made her do that.

We had dinner with Elene and Satyananda. He was thin, almost a waif. He was neatly groomed with shiny white teeth. He smelled of saffron and wore loose pants and a blue silk shirt that seemed to emphasize his thin arms. We told him how grateful we were that he let Elene live with him.

In the months that followed we seemed to be walking passageways between one reality and another. We paid Satyananda $500 a month, but Elene's reality didn't include settling down. She soon reverted to incoherent wandering. We would call Satyananda and Elene would have been gone for several days. Once he thought she was at the River Street Shelter. Or again she was at another man's house, a friend of Satyananda's.

Oh, God, my thoughts would say, what horrible things are happening to her now? Was she in any state of mind that we would recognize? What happened to that child of mine? What should we be doing? Should we coerce her into some facility? We talked with professional after professional and got the same response: she's not endangering others or herself. Until she does, she's a free woman. She has rights, too.

And then she would be back with Satyananda, and we would talk with her and she would ramble on about Micah. When they took him away from her, they destroyed her balance and she could never dance again. Other times she would cry and ask us to send her to Africa where she could live in a village without TVs and computers and microwaves and where they never cut any body hair, never practiced circumcision, where people were born and died in the same house. And when I said I didn't think she'd really like that, she raged that we never understood her and hung up. Next time it would be the Hutterites she wanted to live with. I explained that the Hutterites held strict religious and ethnic boundaries to which she would have trouble subscribing. But she liked their disavowal of TV and their small village ways.

When I said, "Good night," she reacted swiftly. "I don't know what good night means. The words have bad vibrations." I tried to imagine what the Hutterites would make of that idea.

Was there any way to get Elene's reality in sync with the society she lived in?

Karma was now letting her come back to the Boulder Creek house for a few hours at a time, sometimes even sleeping over. That relieved us a bit. We surmised that his purpose was to get the dishes washed, the laundry done, the bathrooms cleaned, and a pot of brown rice cooked. On the other hand, we assumed that Elene appreciated seeing the boys and also liked being needed.

She called us from Boulder Creek. It was about eleven o'clock on Easter morning and we had been to early church. We were having coffee and a hot-cross bun. She was talking fast. "I'm all alone in the house."

"But you're in Boulder Creek. I'm glad to hear that. How are you?"

She began to cry with a long, drawn-out moan. "I've broken some windows."

"Accidents happen. Don't let that upset you."

"No. I broke some windows."

"You did? How?"

"A hammer. Something."

"One window. That's not bad."

"No. Lots of windows. When Karma comes back he'll have me sent away. What can I do?"

"Maybe he'll understand. We can pay for the windows."

I thought, Why are we always paying and thinking that takes care of things? It takes care of so little. How can we expect our pitiful pocketbooks to solve anything? I said, "Why did you do it, Elene?"

"We needed the air. We needed light."

There was a pause. There was fear in her voice. "I hear Karma coming." And she hung up.

Karma called us later. "Elene is in the hospital. She broke our windows. I counted sixty of them."

"Sixty!" I said. "Do you have that many in your house?"

"Some of them are small."

"Have someone come in and replace them. Send us the bill." There I was again, throwing dollars at pain. "I'm so sorry," I said. "It must be hard." I meant that. He certainly must love her, or once have loved her. I was sure she loved him. But I remembered his violence toward her and I remembered the ring down the toilet. I knew that love is as breakable as glass, and though it may be tinged with pain, surely hammers are one of its mortal enemies.

We drove up the next weekend. The miles seemed endless, no beauty in the oaks between Santa Maria and King City, nothing but dragging hours into Salinas. We pretty well knew what to expect and what not to expect in Santa Cruz. We went up the hill into Aptos and along the high ground to Soquel and the hospital. We stopped there before even getting our motel room. Reporting to the desk, the nurse disappeared and came back saying Elene couldn't see us.

"How can that be? We've driven four hundred miles to see her. Tell her."

The nurse came back a second time and leaned over the desk to confide in us. "She can't see you until she has something to give you. She wants to offer you something when you come. Adele's taking care of it. I don't think it'll be too long."

As we sat waiting, staff filtered by. Social workers, nurses, interns—we could say hello to each—Paul, Edgar, Marcella—by now we knew them all. I was searching for words to describe them—noble, dedicated, humane, warm-hearted, decent, unselfish. Daily they faced the doctors on one hand and the patients on the other. The doctors provided the flags and the battle plans; the staff stood on the frontlines and carried the wounded on their backs. I loved them all. Of one thing I was sure—there wasn't a Nurse Ratched among them.

When Adele ushered us in, Elene held out two paper plates with cheesecake. "I wanted to offer you something," she said, her eyes cloudy but pleading and dancing like a sky that couldn't decide whether to rain or shine.

Cheesecake was the last thing my stomach wanted just then, but I would have eaten it all if it killed me.

Elene talked compulsively. "A man was following me. He had a cap pulled down. I walked fast. When I got to the house I locked the door. There was no air. I had to have some. I needed to break those windows. It's terrible here. I have convulsions at night. It's like having a baby. I bite on a towel. Would you send me that little prayer rug that Michael gave me?"

Michael Nickle, I thought. She remembers him. I suppose a woman never forgets her first love, or her first abortion!

We said we'd like to bring the boys to see her.

"I can't see the boys. Don't let them come in."

"Why?"

"They'll be contaminated. My medications seep into my aura. It will contaminate them. I can't see them while I'm in the hospital."

That night we took Karma and the boys to a Mexican restaurant. As I watched the boys eat their enchiladas, I wondered what it would be like to have a mother taken away to a mental hospital. Mothers are meant to be available to cheer goals and patch pains. No one should lock mothers away.

On that visit, we had a long talk with Sam Wurlitz, Elene's new social worker. He looked the Santa Cruz type—beard, open shirt, earrings. His office was disarmingly disorganized. We liked his open friendliness. He had already talked many times with Elene and seemed attuned to her case.

"Her delusional system may be delusional but it's also highly coherent. She's amazing."

That seemed to me a good insight. I said, "Yes. But delusions are still delusions. Where are we going? What's her future? Do you consider her schizophrenic?"

He raised his eyebrows. "Maybe. Probably. Lots of paranoia. In the long run the only hope is for her to realize that she is ill and take those medications."

I knew it was true but somehow it irked me. It was blaming her for her troubles, at least for not taking the meds. "I can sure see why she doesn't want to take them. They make her miserable. She bites a towel for relief. They affect her terribly. And you don't have any pills that make her want to take the other pills."

"We all know that. We live in hope that the drugs will get better."

"What about the short run?" My thoughts had turned to housing.

"She'll get out of the hospital, probably too soon. The patient advocates will arrange a writ of habeas corpus, which means her case will land in the courts. She'll appear before the judge and probably act quite normal. She can do that. She's done it. The judge will read her file perfunctorily. He'll ask if she has a place to live, and a couple of her friends will say she can live with them. The judge will release her from the hospital. It happens all the time."

"How can we avoid that revolving door?"

"I'd like to find some group housing for Elene. There's a county program, but there are some dangers. She'll be largely on her own."

"But she wouldn't be on the streets. The streets are being on your own in the worst sense."

"Elene is an honest and trusting person. She falls in with people who take advantage of her."

We left Wurlitz, hopeful that she had found a good relationship in him.

On that visit we noticed that among her other fears was emerging another deeper one, that of being sent to a long-term locked facility.

Not long after we returned home, Elene appeared before a judge and was released. She moved back with Karma.

Then we had a call in which she blamed us for abandoning her.

My jaw fell and my voice rose. "Elene, what are you talking about? We've never abandoned you. We never will."

She changed the subject. "Karma won't let me stay here for more than an hour or so at a time. I need to find a society where I can live. I can list the things I want and you can see if there's a society like that." And she proceeded to ramble on with her list of requirements. There should be no piercing of skin, no circumcision, no cutting of hair. There should be no divorce. No meat consumed. No TVs, microwaves, smoke alarms, computers. There should be organized schedules, like doing the laundry on Mondays, but no collective beliefs like religion.

As she went on, I sat back and looked over the list. In it were all her dreams of a better life. Here was her version of utopia.

I tried to be realistic. "Elene, I don't think we can find a society anywhere that meets all of these. I think you must learn to compromise. If you can't, then you must realize you are ill."

Maybe that wasn't the right thing to say, because she hung up. I felt awful. I said to Shirley, "That was a call for help and she probably feels she has no place to turn, and I ended up telling her we can't help. What are we going to do?"

The next morning was not much better. She called from Karma's saying he let her stay for a bit. We talked for at least half an hour, but I could hear Karma in the background complaining that she had eaten too much of the salad and the bread. She was saying to me that she needed a regular job with specific instructions and that when she was cleaning the bathroom at Karma's, he turned on the TV and then she couldn't work. And then came an old refrain. The cause of all her trouble was their taking Micah away.

I said, "I know. It must have been so hard, so hard." After a pause I took a new tack. "Surely there are some good things in your life. Tell me about those."

There was another silence, and then she hung up.

That same day we had a note from Oracle written with felt pen in half-inch-high script.

Mr. and Mrs. Hine,
    I am writing to tell you that you must get a place for Elene. She needs a place of her own. You can do this. You have not done right by Elene but I forgive you. I am her father and I am your father, and I forgive you.
One Love, One Light, One Consciousness,
Oracle Abo, Healer

I threw his note in the trash. Oracle, my "father." Thanks, Mr. Oracle, for your forgiveness. Thanks a lot.

But the note did cause us to think that maybe the time had come to bring her back down here to Irvine? Shirley and I hashed over the possibility of getting her a room somewhere near us. But could she stand it away from her boys? And what if she needed hospitalization? We would have robbed her of familiar doctors and an environment where even the police recognize her. The mental health people up there know and like her. Down here nothing like that applies. We might do infinite harm.

The possibility, however, remained in our minds during our Christmas visit. Elene was sleeping in a room at Susan's not far down the road from Karma's. The first night we were there Karma had given Elene two hours at his place.

The evening started beautifully. The Christmas tree was up with decorations that Elene kept faithfully from year to year, some of them from her childhood. How they had survived the giveaway years, I'll never know, but she had remained sentimental about some things. With her precious money she had bought two dozen red rosebuds as a centerpiece for the table.

Elene didn't want to go back that night to Susan's, so we got her a room where we were staying at the Pasatiempo Motel. Gently I broached the subject of her coming down to stay with us or near us for a while. I could sense fear rising in her eyes as she looked at me hard. Then she faced away and said, "I guess that might be a good idea." She felt cornered, I could tell that.

We called right then and made a reservation on our return flight, two days hence.

Elene had no suitcase, so the next morning we picked up the boys and headed for the Capitola mall. It was time for our pre-Christmas tradition of invading the stores, each boy picking out three possibilities, and our returning alone to chose one each for Christmas. That way we knew precisely what they wanted, but still there was a bit of surprise left. Now we had an added purpose at the mall—to pick up a suitcase for Elene.

The Capitola mall was jammed. Children created pandemonium, crying as they pulled boxes from shelves, adults tried helplessly to control, and "Rudolph" blared everywhere. We started at a luggage shop. Elene couldn't decide on a suitcase. Gale began to whine and when I scolded him for whining, Elene got mad.

She screamed over the music, "You don't understand. He's reacting to my going away. You're forcing me into this mall syndrome. I hate malls. I don't need a suitcase. I'll use cardboard boxes."

Shirley tried. "You need something more on the plane."

Elene exploded. "I'd rather hitchhike." She ran out of the store.

I tried to follow, but crowds blocked every turn. For a while we all searched and then with sinking stomachs gave up. We returned to the routine with the boys in the toy stores, but there was little joy left.

No word from Elene all that day. We called Karma and Susan and nothing from them either. The day dragged on. After supper we took the boys home. They seemed unusually withdrawn. At bedtime in the motel we put a note on the room we had rented for Elene, telling her to get the key at the desk, and we told the office to give it to her if she came.

We went to bed and were barely asleep about eleven thirty, when we had a call from Karma. He had Elene on another line and connected us. Elene was at the Capitola mall and asked if we could pick her up at the main entrance. We got cut off, but we assumed she had heard us say that we'd come right away.

We dressed fast and drove down the freeway to Capitola. By then it was after midnight. The stores were all closed and dark except for security lights. We found the main entrance but no Elene. The main doors were still open and we went inside, hurrying through the dark hallways. We stopped isolated janitors. None of them recognized our descriptions. We happened on a lone policeman who helped us search down lonely corridors. He finally told us we'd better give up, that she simply wasn't there. He took our name and motel number in case he came across her.

Back in the car, we drove down every midnight street on which she might have walked to get back to the motel. We tried the bus station where feeble fluorescents lit empty platforms and signs told us the last bus had come and gone. We were cold. I could see Shirley's hands shaking on the steering wheel. We were discouraged. We made our way to the motel, saying little, and went back to bed.

Once asleep again, we had a call from Elene. She was at Karma's. Thinking we had hung up on her and weren't coming, she had taken the last bus of the night from Capitola to downtown Santa Cruz and then walked, yes, walked, nearly ten miles over dark, mountainous roads to Boulder Creek. She expressed no regrets, no resentment, nothing but matter-of-fact acceptance of life as it was. Karma had said she could stay there the rest of the night. We said we'd come up in the morning and returned to bed, spilling out to one another in the dark our measures of sadness and relief.

The next morning at their house, we found Elene babbling in the bathroom, her period having started, blood all over her clothes. She wanted to start packing her things at Susan's, so we threw her clothes in the washer and took her to Susan's.

At Susan's we couldn't get her to start packing. Shirley and I got irked and went outside to wait in the car. "Time," Elene yelled. "That's all you think about. I don't care about time."

It was cold outside and it was getting dark. I felt a sore throat coming on. Damn, I don't need a cold just now. We turned the motor on so we could get some heat. After about an hour, I said to Shirley, "This is ridiculous. Let's go."

Shirley went into Susan's and was gone for at least another half an hour. By then I was sure I was going to have a lulu of a sore throat, so I went in to see what was going on, hoping at least to be in the warm house.

In the room Elene was saying she couldn't go back to that motel. "I hated it. There are smoke alarms in the ceiling. A tiny blue light flashes. I know it's there."

I was getting irritated. "Look, Elene. Smoke alarms are everywhere. They're required by law. We even have them in our rooms at home."

It was the wrong thing to say. Elene picked up on it immediately. "You have them at home?"

"Yes, but they're not very evident."

"Then I can't go there."

Shirley tried to calm things. "Let's talk about this tomorrow. We'll pick up the boys, bring them here, and we can organize from there." We crept out.

I awoke with a full-blown cold. We got to Boulder Creek about nine. Elene was already at Karma's. She had walked from Susan's in the middle of the night and slept on Karma's cold front porch.

Shirley sat beside Elene and listened to her ramble. I took Karma aside and lectured him.

"Look, Karma, Elene is your wife. You're committed to her, like it or not. If you continue to put her out, she'll wander the streets again, and the next thing you know she'll die in some violent way—a car accident, violence from some other street person, who knows. If you really love her, that's not so pretty a picture."

He grunted a "Yeah."

I sneezed and feared any effectiveness I was having was broken by my watering eyes and rasping voice. "The other alternative is to let her come back home. Someday she'll accept proper medication and you two can find some kind of normal life. You have to give her a chance."

Oracle had come in, thrown himself into a chair, and listened while thumbing a magazine. As I was sneezing he was mumbling about the horrors of the medical establishment.

Blowing my nose and looking at Oracle, it flashed through my mind that the street held no horrors for these people; it was the hospital and the medications that held the horrors. This was a different world of priorities and hopes. I thought of Robert Frost's "Birches." Maybe it was my cold suggesting poems about cold places. Maybe it was the slimness of a birch branch, too weak on which to hang hopes. Maybe the chance of Karma taking my advice was about as likely as my arthritic joints riding a birch branch.

But I wanted to be a rider of birches. If only I didn't have this damned cold, maybe I'd be more effective trying to twist Karma's arm into riding birches, too. Could we together bring Elene with us into a cold birch-clad land where there was no need for smoke detectors, where the TVs and the microwaves were hidden in the quaking leaves and everyone had long hair, where each took responsibility for his or her own life, doing what had to be done and facing what had to be faced? I, too, would like to be a swinger of birches.

Chapter Twelve

Double Doors on a Thousand Nights

Our close friends and neighbors, Don and Phyllis, heard it all. Shirley and I told it to them in excruciating detail, year after year, and I wondered if the incessant refrain didn't nearly break up our friendship. I've read in their eyes and even heard them say, "Get on with your lives. You've done all you can. It's enough. More is too much."

But we didn't stop retelling our stories to them. In the next two years we unburdened on them more of Elene's wanderings, of her missing Gale's tenth birthday party on a windy day in the park, of her throwing rocks at polluting cars, of a midnight call from Park City, Utah, where on a countercultural jaunt Elene had asked to be let out of a van because the men were smoking, and where she spent ten days in the local hospital before she was flown back to the care of her Santa Cruz social worker.

That last episode began another stay in Dominican. After that she lived for a while in an apartment near Eastcliff where its smoke detector ended in pieces and its windows were broken to let out the fumes and the fears.

Shirley and I had taken each of these happenings one by one. They defined our life but did not consume it. No one raises a child without rocks on the path, and these were the ones we were faced with. We never doubted that hemophilia, if we had chosen that path, would have thrown up just as many stumbling stones. And we never doubted that love for our child would guide us, and we assumed that same love, whatever the contours of her minds, made a difference for her, too.

We knew Don and Phyllis, as well as other friends and even my brother, were calling us Pollyannaish, patsies, hopeless romantics. They would pull out the "tough love" arguments, even the rights of parents to face old age in peace. We didn't accept any of those nostrums. Sometimes we even resented hearing them, because none of them described for us the loving parents of a schizophrenic child. In effect we lived two lives—our Riverside or Irvine life and our Santa Cruz life. They were two separate stages, two separate plays, and the characters in one didn't have to, and perhaps couldn't, understand the others.

Calls from Elene continued to be filled with alarms. She said she was aging too fast. She was facing death and she dwelt on dying. She was afraid dying would feel like being confined in that historic contraceptive corset she had seen in a museum in England. (What a memory for details of twenty years ago!) She roamed on through flights of words about her eyes on fire when she inadvertently watched TV with the boys, about a tiny baby on some man's finger, about her ovaries hot and melting.

She was back in the hospital. We talked with the doctor. He said they were trying Trilafon.

We drove up. It was the Memorial Day weekend. We sat with Elene in the visiting section at Dominican. We noticed right away her stooped shoulders, eyes nearly closed, shuffling gait, tremors, pasty hands and stiff neck. In slurred speech she told us her eyes wouldn't focus for reading. I could only hope that as bad as it was, maybe it wasn't as bad as Haldol.

To avoid some cigarette smoke Elene asked us to her room. Her roommate wasn't in. The room was intensely tidy, bed made, bowl clean, hairbrush and comb in place.

"Locked facilities are terrible," Elene said even before we were seated. She pushed her long hair back with a trembling hand and looked toward the window. The curtains made the bars beyond barely visible.

"You've had good help from this place through the years," Shirley said, obscuring the fact that we knew "this place" was not in the category of a long-term locked facility, which implied years taken from a life, not a week or two.

She said, "Harbor Hills has drugs and people get violent."

I had always assumed that Elene was nowhere near one of those long-term stereotypical snake pits where they threw away the key.

"You're not going to any such place," Shirley said. She leaned over to give Elene a hug. Elene dodged her and ran out the door. We followed her but couldn't find her. We waited a bit in the visiting section, and I thought of this newer fear. Elene had so many fears—smoke alarms, pollution, hospital conspiracies, microwaves, TV, cameras—and now these were overridden by the fear of a locked facility.

Eventually we told the nurses to tell Elene we had left, that we loved her, and that we'd be back tomorrow.

It was early afternoon, so we stopped in the county offices to see if Elene's social worker was busy. He wasn't. After the amenities, we asked about long-term locked facilities. He pushed back in his chair and combed his long hair with his fingers. "That's a doctor's call. Sometimes when Dominican gets overburdened and the locked facilities have space, the doctors are tempted."

"Elene is desperately afraid of that."

"You must realize that we all feel some perplexity in the handling of Elene. She's too well educated, too well read to be comfortable in the company of most mentally ill. For example, I think she uses her aversion to smoking as a screen for that feeling of incompatibility. She can't relate to them and smoking says that to her. That's her problem in the hospital. Her knowledge of technology has led to a fear so great that it outweighs any benefits the medicines and hospitals give her."

I had to digest that, but it seemed perceptive.

A few days later we returned home, assuming Elene would be at Dominican until she could go again to SART for a few weeks, and then Karma might take her back or the county might find good housing.

What happened was far different. On the Thursday before the Labor Day weekend, Elene's social worker called to tell us that she had been transferred to a long-term locked facility.

"Oh, God," I said to him. "It's happened."

He went on fast. "But it's not Harbor Hills. It's a much better place, the San Jose Care and Guidance Facility."

My first thought was that San Jose was so far from her boys. He gave us the San Jose phone number and we called immediately, dreading that we would hear Elene incoherent or in tears. To our great surprise, she calmly said she'd like us to visit, partly because we could get her own toothbrush and her own underwear.

The next day we were early on the road and got to San Jose in the late afternoon. We found San Jose Care and Guidance on the far edge of town near the brown hills that rimmed the southeast side of the Bay. The place was a spreading one-story building in a sparsely populated area with swinging glass doors at the front. We were admitted by a receptionist and then waited for an attendant to unlock the inside door. We were told to sit in a small, utilitarian, antiseptic room with a dozen plastic chairs and a round table with piles of ripped, ancient magazines. A Mexican family, an older man and woman and a young man, maybe eighteen, were sitting in the opposite corner. We nodded hello and the older ones nodded back. We sat in our corner and picked up a magazine that we had no intention of reading. The Mexican family wasn't talking. The mother looked occasionally to the young man and smiled while he smiled weakly back and then turned his eyes to the courtyard.

Eventually locks turned on inner doors and Elene was ushered in. She reluctantly allowed us to hug her. Her hair was a bit stringy and her eyes were dazed, but she looked far better than I had expected.

We were full of questions. "How do you like this place?"

"There's a piano in the recreation room."

That sent my tensions down a notch. I noticed the Mexican mother and father leaving and the boy ringing at the inside door for a nurse to take him back.

"Is the food good?"

"I trade meat for veggies. The cook gives me Chinese fragrant rice. Could you bring me some blackstrap molasses and some olive-sesame oil?"

140

"Of course, we'll bring it over from Santa Cruz when we come tomorrow."

"Are they going to tie my tubes?"

Shirley was shaking her head. "I'm sure they won't do that."

"When I'm asleep they might."

She was beginning to pace back and forth. "I can't see the boys. They'll be contaminated."

I was bemoaning to myself the number of fears she bore, but we talked on, constantly trying to reassure her. She told us she needed Tom's natural toothpaste. That plus the olive-sesame oil would take away the pain of her back molar, which had been aching for a week or so.

When the nurse took her back, I watched through the wired glass panel in the locked door as she shuffled down the long, dreary corridor of vinyl tiles and doors on either side. The wire in the glass acted like fresh crushed onions before my eyes. I thought about how lonely she must feel—loneliness and boredom, the great burdens of mental illness. They were the terrible price she was paying for survival. The triangles of the wired window framed her, walking alone, probably trembling.

Driving over the mountain to Santa Cruz, we felt pretty low. Since it was the Labor Day weekend, we knew there would be no doctors to answer our questions, though we had plenty of them. What did the future hold now? Would she be in this new facility for the rest of her life? Could we find a better place for the long term? Why the abrupt move from Dominican? Why did they send her to San Jose where it would be hard for the boys to visit her? And we knew our questions would lie there like limp fish through Labor Day.

We spent the evening with Gale and Jonathan, and the next morning we picked up the molasses and sesame oil, poured the contents into plastic bottles (we had been warned—no glass), and headed back to San Jose. When the three of us were settled in the waiting room, Elene's talk was still delusional, but she seemed sweet and adaptable, and her usual furrowed forehead occasionally broke into a weak smile. She was visibly pleased with the blackstrap and oil. I kept thinking over and over that she was a true survivor, that she had faced another dragon, the long-term locked facility, and that she was about to tame this one, too.

That night we bought the boys some clothes, took them to our motel for the night, swam with them, and admired their new diving skills as they retrieved coins from the bottom. We saw a movie, *Three Ninjas* (awful, but the boys loved it). We slept together in one room; that is, we eventually slept, after the boys' endless giggles, tricks, and our grandparental efforts at quieting.

The morning after the holiday, we got together with Sam Wurlitz, her social worker, and Robert Goldstein, her new conservator from the public guardian's office. We were surprised to learn that neither of them felt that Elene should have been sent to a long-term facility. Dr. Luther had been on vacation and his associate, Dr. Katz, had been adamant. He felt that Elene would profit from long-term treatment, but Wurlitz and Goldstein admitted that Katz might have acted in light of a serious space problem at Dominican.

They were reassuring that the San Jose facility was among the best, far better than Harbor Hills, and Elene would get good care there. They advised us to let matters rest until Elene's scheduled court hearing on a permanent conservatorship. If during the hearing, Goldstein felt things were going badly for Elene's possible long-term commitment, he would request a continuance to allow us, the parents, to investigate private therapy.

We took their advice, not knowing where we were headed, but feeling any other option, such as protesting to Dr. Katz, would be counterproductive.

Later that day when we saw Elene in her dreary visiting room, we told her of our day with the boys, their new swimming skills, the coins in the pool, and the movie. Her usual worried frown lit up in smiles. We could tell how hungry she was to see them. How long, I thought, in the deadness of confinement could she get along without hugging them, putting them to bed, washing their clothes? Those eight- and ten-year-olds were the chief if not the only joy of her life. Their heartbeats were hers, too. The thought of her crumpling pain clawed within me. What could San Jose Care and Guidance do to compensate?

The director was back that day and showed us around. It made us feel a bit better. The total facility was not bad, just institutional. And we knew Elene had a marvelous capacity for adaptation. The director explained a system of rewards so that points for good conduct (like cooperation or attendance at therapy sessions) led to passes for group walks in parks or town, shopping, even movies (with attendants). When we came, she might get day passes so we could drive her over the mountain to Santa Cruz for time with the boys. The picture became a bit less bleak.

Going home on that long stretch between Salinas and King City, the usual wind propelled us south like the world's sad undertow. Shirley and I were unusually silent. I think we were unable to verbalize our tangled emotions of disappointment and helplessness. I looked out at the stooping laborers in the latticed lettuce fields and wondered how many of them were bearing similar burdens.

Shirley broke the silence. "That place is remarkably clean. It smelled good."

I added weakly, "The fragrant rice and the piano are plusses."

Then we were quiet again, neither wanting to talk about long-term confinement.

Actually we should have known better than to get too down. Elene has internal resources beyond belief. Initially she was unhappy at San Jose Care. How could she be otherwise? She wanted to play the piano late at night and that was not allowed. In the daytime when she could play the piano, Ping-Pong players were close by, laughing and screaming. As usual, most of the patients and many of the nurses smoked, and though they had to go to specific places for smoking, Elene could smell the tobacco on their clothes and breath.

Nevertheless, Elene's bounce-back abilities never failed. There was a patient advocate, as in all such facilities, and Elene was able to convince that woman that she was not a proper candidate for long-term incarceration. Since she already had her social worker and her conservator thinking that way, it wasn't long before the doctors and administrators followed suit.

On September 25, 1992, we received a perfectly rational note from Elene:

Dear M and Papa,

There has been a change of plan and probably next week I will be moved to SART in Santa Cruz for three weeks, have my dental work taken care of while I am there, and they will gradually ease me off medication under the supervision of Dr. Luther. If this works out, I will be very glad.

Love,

Elene

By the end of September she was transferred back to SART.

The San Jose experience, however, could hardly be expunged. There lurked in our minds the lingering thought that maybe sometime Elene would need long-term care and that possibly she would be denied public facilities or we would find the public facilities unacceptable. She was, after all, an unusual person, one who did not fit into many situations. For one example, her diet concerns were not amenable to most group kitchens. Shouldn't we be prepared with private alternatives?

So we began calling professionals and compiling a file of mental health homes. Most were clearly wrong either in philosophy, dietary approaches, or location. But we did come across one that seemed good: Hambleceya, in Lemon Grove, near San Diego. It emphasized natural foods, gave the patients lots of responsibility, de-emphasized technology such as microwaves, and tolerated very little TV.

Shirley and I drove down to Hambleceya in early October. It was in a somewhat rural setting, a big, two-story, 1930s stucco house with several added rooms over the garage. The garden included lawns, flowerbeds, and a vegetable plot. About a dozen patients lived there with a small staff, including Dr. Fitzpatrick whom we talked with and liked. As we were being shown around, a group of patients in a van returned from a field trip. They appeared lively and happy. I could see real possibilities here.

We paid a refundable deposit at Hambleceya and got plane schedules to bring Elene down to check it out. When we broached the idea to Elene, there were a few moments when she seemed no more than cool and the possibility was there. But then she reared back.

"No. I can't leave Santa Cruz. I can't leave my boys, seeing them as often as I can."

"Karma might not let you live there."

"He will. I love him. He knows that. I'll go back to my Eastcliff apartment and work things out from there."

Our Hambleceya castle collapsed. When the doctors released Elene from SART, she fell in with Shirley Chang, a diplomate in acupuncture who initiated various herbal therapies. In the tangled thicket of Elene's mind two strong vines continued to thrive. She wanted to be near her boys but at the same time she wanted to get far away to some Shangri-la where all her desires and presumed needs would be observed. In this next phase of her life, it was the latter compulsion that dominated. It became a desperate search. She wanted to come down to Irvine so we could help her, but now, suddenly, she would not accept any money from us. She claimed our money always led to misfortune. Given her life thus far, I could hardly argue with her.

Then in early December came a frantic call. Her keys had been stolen and she was convinced someone planned to break into her apartment and attack her. She was terrified to spend another night in that place. She was coming down on the night bus to Irvine and would arrive early next morning. It was only kind fortune that did not allow Shirley and me to foresee what the next two weeks would be like.

We met her at the bus depot, her hair unfettered, her dress long and faded, her gait halting because the strap on one of her sandals was broken. Her small backpack held jars of sprouts and molasses, but no change of clothes.

It was the first time she had been to our retirement community in Irvine. I watched her roam quietly through our apartment, looking at old photographs on the walls and touching familiar objects like our Gump's jade Ming tree or the red fired-clay bird she had made in the second grade. We ate a quiet lunch in our place—sliced tomatoes and bean sprouts with mozzarella cheese and vinaigrette. Afterward Shirley suggested they shop for clothes, and, miracle of miracles, the idea worked. Three or four hours later they returned with skirts, a shirt, a sweater, and new sandals. That night Shirley confided that to see Elene decide on such things and actually let us buy them for her was mind-boggling.

For dinner we went downstairs to the dining room. Elene was charming. Some friends came by to meet her, and when two of them asked if she had children, she told them not only about Gale and Jonathan but also about Micah. She spared no details—he was fathered by a friend of her husband's and the authorities had taken the baby away from her. Leaving the dining room, she removed her new sandals and walked upstairs barefoot.

In the night several times I heard her cry out, "Help!" The next morning she was vague and delusional. She seemed obsessed with what had gone wrong with her life and the explanations came pouring out—being taken from her mother where she would have been breast fed; being forced to eat regularly; having been incarcerated in mental hospitals simply for breaking windows; having been drugged in the hospitals secretly at night; having her pubic hair cut; having squished with her finger a daddy longlegs under a soap dish. She was sure her boys had been irreparably damaged by being allowed sugared drinks as they watched TV. These were her signposts on a life gone wrong. She was fearful of women who used douches, of men who were circumcised, of anyone who had allowed parts of their bodies to be cut off. "By twenty-three," she said, "I had had all the experiences in life I wanted."

Underlying these explanations, I detected certain logic, because before breakfast was over, she was back to the reason she had given us for coming down. She wanted my help in finding somewhere in the world where she could be happy. Could I help her with a letter that she could send to countries throughout the world? She proposed that she dictate and I type out her needs. I said it would be easy on the computer. She thought for a long time.

"I can't sit by a computer. Could I sit around the corner in the next room?"

"Sure, why not? As long as I can hear you."

This is the letter that resulted. I typed verbatim, clarifying some syntax as I went.

I am trying to find a place where the following things are available. Is it possible that your country would provide any or all of them?

Since I was separated from my third child, I make different movement patterns, consisting mainly of dance forms from other countries and consequently I have been persecuted by placing me in asylums and jails. I therefore seek some kind of political asylum. I want to live in a country where such patterns will be acceptable.

I gave birth to my children with a midwife, not doctor. Movements were not restricted during labor. I ate placenta after birth so that I would equate childbearing with increased nutritional balance. I breast-fed my babies on demand.

I look for a place where safety comes from having more children rather than from having a job. I want having children to be economically responsible. I want living to be multi-generational, people living with next of kin for the longest possible time. [There was a lump in my throat as I typed those words.]

I want an area where petrochemicals are seen as an ecological problem. I have tried to be more energy efficient, but have been interfered with when my child had blood withdrawn and was injected with antibiotics. Most societies are not geared around large families. They are trying to reduce family size. This frightens me because in larger families each member has a different role and the advantage of a small family gives energy. Separating family members by birth control dissipates that energy. It is a dissolute society when they absorb the energy into diversions and social practices that do not result in procreation.

Society keeps people dissolute by forcibly separating family members from one another and not allowing them to pursue repetitive movement patterns that they are familiar with. They then seek out other movement patterns so they can channel the enormous energy and so get free labor out of the population. I disagree with this because this free labor is tied into industry that is ecologically unsound.

I want to make as many movements as possible while consuming as few nutrients as possible. This society is doing the opposite. It is oriented on signs of privilege that are unconnected with increased family size, and I think it should be the reverse.

After giving birth, the mother's separation from the infant, for no matter how short a time, causes the loss of additional strength and adaptability gained from giving birth (if movements weren't restricted in the birth).

So I would like to live in a community that is interested in exploring this God-given resource of strength, adaptability, and learning capacity that comes from families adding members without having their movement patterns restricted. The family should channel the energy and the adaptability and the learning capacity into work of the family's own choosing.

I could tell she was getting edgy and I was getting tired, too. I glanced over the letter. What an amazing collection of words and ideas! I thought of Wurlitz's comment that she didn't have much in common with most mentally ill people. Maybe she doesn't have much in common with most people in general. She wants to keep her children; she wants a big family, extended ad infinitum. She wants natural childbirth. She wants ecological balance. I puzzled over the references to blood and body parts and repetitive movements and energy and free labor, but they were only details in her dreams for family, community, and environment. I closed my eyes and said to myself, "God give us more delusions." And I opened my eyes and said, "Alas, that isn't the world we live in, and God help us if we can't live in this world."

Even though Shirley was cooking big pots of steamed vegetables, Elene was not eating. The next day Elene was unusually depressed and delusory. Other elements in the general picture didn't help. Shirley came down with a cold, and my back went out. The rain poured down outside. It was a day to chant an elegy on why.

Elene was now talking incessantly, making little sense, and that afternoon her period began. She had no underpants or pads, and she wouldn't use Shirley's, so we did our best with towels and old padding on the bed and chairs. I ignored my aching back and tried to raise spirits by working on the letter and duplicating it for foreign countries. But Elene had lost interest. She now wanted to go back to Santa Cruz.

In the following days she ate less and less. As Shirley washed sheets and bloody towels every morning, we watched Elene growing more and more lethargic. We had to do something, and our decision was to get her back to Santa Cruz. That might snap her out of it, or if she was heading for the hospital, that was the right place to be. So we bought plane tickets, rounded up our things, and with Elene hardly aware of what was happening, we taxied to the airport and boarded the plane.

Elene sat between us, nearly paralyzed with fright. Technology was here in command and we were its innocent victims, bound in its tentacles, roaring to destruction. I held her hand and it was wet with sweat. She looked straight ahead with a kind of stoic determination, and I could see the muscles in her jaw flexing. The flight was, mercifully, only one hour.

From San Jose in a rented car Shirley drove us over the mountain in a pouring rain. Elene said she wanted to go to her place rather than be at the motel with us so we took her to her room on Eastcliff. That was the first time we had been inside the room. It was depressingly small, hardly bigger than the futon bed on the floor. No furniture, only piles of clothes, papers, and packages of half-eaten food. She said she wanted to sleep and crawled under some crumpled blankets on the futon. By then it was early evening, but with the rain outside, it seemed dark enough that she might sleep through the night.

We told her we'd be at our usual Comfort Inn and quietly closed the door.

In the motel Shirley and I organized ourselves and when we were ready for bed, there was a knock on the door. It was Elene, dripping and disheveled, having walked all the way in the rain. "I can't stay in that room. The smoke detector is working again. And someone has my keys. They could get in any time."

We got her in the hot shower, Shirley gave her one of her nightgowns, and we bedded down for the night, three of us in two queen-size beds.

The next day, the sun shining, and with a bit of breakfast in all of us, we set out on a search for a new room or apartment. Elene liked nothing we saw. By then it was afternoon and the boys would be home from school, so we headed for Boulder Creek.

The boys knew that this was our Christmas visit and we should go to the stores to make lists. When we walked in, Karma seemed mildly happy to see Elene. When we explained we'd been looking for a new apartment, he said, as if it were an accusation, why doesn't she stay here? He had relented. I felt as if a taut, twisted muscle had just relaxed.

We told the boys to get ready and asked Elene if it wouldn't be easier to take the boys alone.

Somehow that set her off. Who knows whether she was nervous at the thought of being left alone with Karma after his long negative streak or if some synapse had snapped, who knows? But she blew up. She yelled that she would not trust her boys with us. She started berating Shirley, calling her selfish, and crying that Shirley had never been any good as a mother. She blamed Shirley's artificial hips. Then she said it was the metal bridgework in her teeth. She yelled that Shirley should take out her bridge right now. That's what was needed to make her a good mother again. She lunged at Shirley, trying to get at her mouth, and her nails scratched Shirley's cheek until it bled. She was apparently trying to save Shirley from some dire fate. Karma and I pulled her away. Shirley ran to the car, locked herself in, and cried bitterly. By then Gale was crying, too, sure that now they couldn't go for their Christmas lists. It was a miserable moment.

It's never possible for me to say how those storms pass, but like the heavenly storms, they do. We managed to get the boys in the car. They each gave Shirley big hugs. We took them alone for their Christmas lists and for a matinee movie, Disney's *Aladdin*.

That night Gale's school class was to lead the La Posada parade from the old mission down through the Garden Mall. So we took them to the parade's gathering place at the mission Adobe. We all stood around bonfires, drank chocolate, and made *luminarias*.

I could hardly believe my eyes when I saw Karma and Elene arrive. Elene smiled, said hello, and acted as if nothing had happened. We were all bundled up from the cold, but I could see that her hazel eyes, reflecting the firelight, were bright.

Since Shirley and I couldn't take the long walk, we agreed to meet them at the end of the parade route and they all went off carrying their *luminarias* and singing "O Come All Ye Faithful." We, too, were settling back into joyful and triumphant.

We left the next day. The buzzing of the plane's motor kept reminding me of the Arabian Nights. Even Disney couldn't harm that compelling story. I suddenly felt that we were a part of those hundreds of generations who have listened to Sinbad and Scheherazade, who have silently borne travails through a thousand and one nights and more. With them all we, too, want to find our magic lamp; we, too, call for that genie to help us. On that plane I knew exactly what I would ask the genie. I would ask for a magic cure for schizophrenia. I would ask for my daughter back, the daughter who drew like a Leonardo and played like a Horowitz. She was right there, right there for the genie to touch. And then the genie would make it possible for Shirley and Elene and me to have three-cornered hugs, and we could talk like adults, laugh and violently disagree without feeling we were walking on eggs.

But if I knew then what I know now, my conversation with the genie wouldn't be the same. I would be far more specific. I would ask it for effective but nondisturbing drugs, for doctors who had time and inclinations to explore dreams and deepest psyches, for my own physical strength to be always there along with Shirley and to cope. Those would be my three wishes for the genie.

Chapter Thirteen

Roots in Rootlessness

Elene was not so much in a revolving door (in and out of the hospital) as on a mystifying ride that took her into a tunnel of estrangement where men drifted like ghosts in and out of her life until the tracks threw her back into the hospital. Usually the hospital was Dominican, but twice the tracks led to another, a long-term facility. And on one occasion when the tracks led her to another visit to Irvine, we nearly joined her in the tunnel.

After Christmas Elene was missing again. On our trip in February 1993, we couldn't find her at her apartment, but we left our motel number on the door. In the motel the next morning, the phone rang. A man introduced himself as Clint Stevens. He said he and Elene were in room 228 and where were we? He and Elene had come last night and been told we were in 228. (Our room was 128 immediately beneath.) They had knocked at 228, pushed open the door, which by some quirk was unlocked, and found us not there. Expecting us to come anytime, they stayed for the night. I could hardly believe it, but he said they thought the lack of luggage or any evidence of our having been in 228 simply meant we hadn't yet arrived but were due soon. All the time we were waiting in our room directly beneath.

So this stranger, Clint Stevens, appeared at our door. He was tall and thin, bearded, and blue-jeaned with a languid voice. Elene followed, and I could tell she was pretty far gone. She beamed but talked incessantly, something about our coming as a put-up job. She was barefoot.

They poured out their story of wondering where we had been all that time. I couldn't bring myself to the obvious questions—why hadn't they asked the desk, why had they waited so long, why hadn't they realized? We could excuse Elene. But this man? Where does his mind come from?

We took them to a vegetarian restaurant. Elene mostly ignored her bowl of chili, smiling warmly at us and often compulsively getting up and wandering. Since she had no shoes, we tried to get her some, but we couldn't get her out of the car. Clint Stevens tried, too, and he seemed understanding, protective, and solicitous.

They went off together but returned the next morning. Elene thought she would like to get some clothes, and that prospect always delighted us. She had in mind a store called Khyber Pass on Telegraph Avenue in Berkeley. Because she needed clothes so badly, we were willing to make the trip.

Clint Stevens wanted to go with us. He had been a good influence on Elene at the shoe stores. Maybe he could be more successful than we were in convincing her to decide on clothes. We took a chance on Clint.

Black, threatening clouds were piling up in the north as the four of us set out on the hour-and-a-half drive to Berkeley. The two young ones sat in the backseat, and in my passenger seat I could hear them clearly.

Clint was talking to her about his youth. Elene must have been looking at our AAA sticker on the windshield. Out of the blue she said, "There are two kinds of people in the world, those who join AA and those who join the AAA. Some join both AA and AAA. Those are the ones to look out for." That comment bore no relationship to Clint's conversation, but standing alone it made wonderful sense.

In the Khyber Pass Elene paced up and down the aisles and could find nothing she liked. Clint kept holding things up and saying, this looks cool. But only no's from Elene. We roamed through other Telegraph Avenue shops, the wild and the weird, clothes from everywhere. Once she ran out of the store. Clint started after her and we told him to meet us at the Bateau Yvre, a cafe we had liked in years past, not far down the street. We thanked our stars for having Clint with us. On our own we would never have found Elene. It began to rain. At the Bateau Yvre there was a fire blazing and we settled down with a bowl of hot onion soup.

Half an hour later, they stumbled in, wet and smiling. Clint ate a lunch worthy of a longshoreman. Elene had only hot milk.

Empty-handed, we drove home in a downpour. I listened to the backseat conversation. Clint dwelt over and over on cars, the Mercedes, the Hummer, the Rolls-Royce he had owned, the speeds he could achieve. Elene never picked up on his bombast, talking of the rain outside, the color of the streams on the window, the clouds over the wild sea. I concluded they had little in common. Was this Clint a leech on Elene?

When we got back to Santa Cruz, we let Clint off at a friend's place, and I felt relieved—not because I disliked him, I just thought he was completely wrong for Elene.

We were still getting ourselves reorganized at the motel and Elene was in the shower when Clint knocked at the door. This time I told him no, that Elene would stay with us for now. He melted back into the rainy night. It was the last time I would talk to Clint Stevens, but far from the last time I would think about him.

The next morning Elene wouldn't wash or comb her hair, and she was, of course, barefoot. We were to fly home that afternoon and presumed we could get Elene settled back on Eastcliff before we left. We proposed using the time for clothes shopping, but Elene vetoed that. Throwing an apple bite at me, she said, "You can't choose my clothes. You're no help." I could tell a rough time was ahead.

Grocery shopping seemed more or less acceptable. While we were waiting in the car for the Staff of Life market to open, conversation got increasingly tense. Elene in the backseat was growing verbally belligerent. First she knocked off my cap and yanked at my hair, saying I had to let it grow so it wouldn't turn so gray. If I let my hair grow, I'd get back my strength.

Then she turned to Shirley's hair, pulled it hard, and yelled something I couldn't understand. Shirley screamed and got out of the car. "Robert," she cried, "We're crazy to put up with this." In tears she walked up the street.

Elene, suddenly quiet and sweet again, asked, "What's the matter with Mom?" I said, "Let's shop." In the market I followed her with a cart. She couldn't decide on anything, just talked constantly. So as we walked I threw in bread, tea, applesauce, popcorn, fruit, carrots, and a lot of vegetarian basics.

When we got back to the car, Shirley was again in the driver's seat. We said little 'til we got to the Eastcliff apartment. I was starting to unload the grocery bags, but Elene was not budging from the backseat. "I can't go in there." Then she burst out of the car and ran off, disheveled and barefoot, around the corner and out of sight. It started to rain again. We waited for a while in the car in the rain.

We found the manager and left the bags of groceries with her; we also left a long note on Elene's door, saying we were sorry to have to leave but to remember we always loved her.

At the motel we called her social worker, Sam Wurlitz, once more enlisting his help. We related the whole weekend story. He knew Clint Stevens and described him as "not mean, just innocently sleazy." Wurlitz said he would take care of things, and we felt only a bit glum as we drove in the rain to San Jose and our plane.

Our lives in Irvine weren't going too smoothly either. Shirley was suffering increasing pain in her legs. The pains streaked down her thigh into the lower leg. She did not walk happily, but she gritted her way along, and in March we flew to Santa Cruz for the boys' birthdays. Elene still was ostensibly on Eastcliff, though seldom there. Wurlitz said he was planning another place for her, assuming we were willing to pay $500 a month rent, which, of course, we agreed to. Alas, at Jonathan's birthday party in the park, replete with cake and ice cream and water guns, Elene did not appear.

Between then and Grandparents' Day at the boys' school in May, Elene had come back to Karma's for a while before he put her out again. Wurlitz's house for her was not materializing. Oracle entered the picture once more and tried to find her a place, but basically Elene was wandering again. The second night we were there for Grandparents' Day, Karma called to say that

Elene had been hanging out in the triangle park across from the Staff of Life market.

Shirley and I drove down there. It was a small park, and if we placed our car strategically we could see the whole triangle. It was about four in the afternoon with a light rain falling. We waited for an hour or two and saw only three homeless men with hoods pulled for the rain. We went off for a quick Chinese dinner, then returned to the park, waiting again, hoping but vaguely dreading. We had brought some takeout food—egg foo yong and cashews with broccoli—for Elene. Silly, wasn't it? But we thought we might find her and she would eat. We finally left the food, wrapped carefully, on a wet bench in the park and returned to the motel.

About eleven thirty that night, a knock on our door. Elene's voice was calling, "Papa." When I got there, still pulling on a shirt and pants, I found her in wet clothes, saying she wanted to get to Boulder Creek so she could go to Grandparents' Day tomorrow.

"Stay here tonight and we'll take you. It'll work fine."

She said something about Ian and Casey and disappeared around the corner of the building. We assumed she was coming back. In time I went out, but she was nowhere to be seen. I walked over to the office and asked them to give her a room if she returned. We went back to bed.

The next morning early she called from a pay phone, saying she was coming over for a ride to Grandparents' Day. That made us feel good, and we waited and waited. It was getting near time for the opening events, so we got in the car near the motel entrance so we could sweep her up and go.

Elene appeared across the street with three men. They bore all the trappings of homelessness—unshaven, torn and baggy pants, even a shopping cart of belongings covered with newspapers for the rain. Weren't they all candidates for the hospitals Reagan closed to save tax money? We drove across the street and asked Elene to hop in the car. We should have known it wouldn't be that easy.

Elene looked at the car and kept repeating, "It isn't right."

The man nearest her, who in passing introduced himself as Casey, gently took her by the arm and motioned to the car, but Elene resisted.

"I'm going on the bus," she said, looking at him imploringly.

In her purse Shirley had a string of green and blue cloisonné beads that my aunt had made for Elene.

"In case we don't see you, Aunty wanted you to have these."

It was wise of Shirley to give Elene the beads there because we never saw her again on that trip. We knew the boys were expecting us at Grandparents' Day. Our obligations turned to them, but at the school as we toured their classroom, admired their drawings, listened to their singing, I kept hoping Elene would come wearing those green and blue beads. They would reflect her hazel eyes like the cool, soothing balm of redwood trees that shiver in the wind.

Home again, with the pain in Shirley's legs coming and going, we had a call from Elene that she had been in San Francisco with Casey, had lost her backpack, and had been arrested. We assumed for loitering, but she would tell us no more. The next day she bashed in Karma's windshield with some blunt object. Oracle was there and called the police and Elene was back in Dominican. When Oracle told us, he said, "It makes me feel very sad."

We called Dr. Luther who said he had her on Navane again, and she was doing better. I pictured that little blue pill that now must be so familiar to her and so dreaded. He said she was remarkably cheerful, speaking gratefully of the hospital as a refuge. "Elene is a remarkable woman. I know few if any other patients who have the ability to find good in practically everything."

He went on to tell us of an experience she had mentioned to him. When she was in San Francisco, she was sleeping on the street over a heating grate. She told him the art deco building across the way was such a lovely sight. It was a place for human beings to gather and they could find better lives that way.

In my mind I could see her face brighten, her hazel eyes, her wrinkled up, smiling nose as she contemplated human beings gathering to make better lives, and all the while she herself was sleeping on a steel grate for warmth on an alien street. Was it her illness that enabled her to see beyond immediate reality into some ultimate meaning? If so, a gift was granted along with the curse.

A few days later Elene called from the hospital to wish Shirley a happy Mother's Day. Shirley thought she sounded wonderful. I entered in my journal: "Glory be."

The next time we heard from her she was crying, having just learned she was going back to a long-term facility. She sobbed as she guessed she would have to end her life in a locked facility. I tried to be reassuring. I said they hadn't kept her there last time. Why should they now? I repeated my feelings about her bravery, how courageous she had been in the past, how much I admired and loved her. She said she had only been able to make it because we had stuck with her, and that brought a lump in my throat. Then she said she wanted to read again. I had not heard that desire for a long time.

"We can send some books. What do you want us to send?"

"I'd like to read some more of Carson McCullers. I remember liking her."

Barnes and Noble, here we come. Give us every Carson McCullers title you've got and put them all in a big jiffy bag. We want to send them off right away.

During this hospitalization, Elene's penchant for making lists and plans blossomed. She sent them to me for my advice. The first one was headed: My Need for Balance.

1) Find additional games I like besides Chinese checkers
2) Family to movies together
3) Disneyland
4) Florida for Disneyworld
5) Camping
6) Bike riding
7) Bookstores
8) Day hikes
9) Beach

There was a list of Career Plans:

1) Housecleaning business
2) Volunteer at library

3) Library clerk
4) Children's librarian
5) Institute for Research in Tropical Medicine

Another was titled Saving for Specials:

1) Furniture
2) Family Vacations
3) Car
4) Christmas
5) Print of Monet's "Le Regence"
6) Art cabinet
7) Wrappings for presents
8) Memories chest
9) Linen chest
10) Individual massage sessions
11) Blankets
12) Wool underwear
13) Watch
14) Wedding ring
15) Bicycle
16) Piano
17) Items to smell good
18) Whole wheat fig bars for snacks

I read the lists over and over. I could see in them the hopes for an organized life, a life of pattern and routine with family movies and day hikes, of dreams for whole wheat fig bars as well as a piano, of existence extending beyond Chinese checkers into a housecleaning business, of the restoration of a wedding ring that had once been thrown down the toilet. Everywhere the hope for a smooth, ordered life against the reality of gritty chaos.

When the expected times at the long-term facility and SART were completed, a halcyon period followed in which orderliness seemed to prevail over chaos. Wurlitz kept promising group housing that was coming up in the county's mental health plans, but it wasn't coming soon. Instead we found Elene a promising place. It was the back lower level of a house on Bear Creek Road, about half a mile from Karma and the boys. It was two rooms, bath, and utility kitchen with big windows looking out on a forest. Elene was delighted, especially with the prospect of the boys biking down to visit. By the first of June she had moved in, renewed her driver's license, and was driving the old green Buick. I worried about that, but I had no power to stop her.

In early July Karma called. He said Elene was off her medications. He had asked her to take her car and go home one night and she had (he claimed deliberately) plowed into a cement post and smashed his garage door. He drove her in the bashed car to her place and told her he didn't want to see her again. He told us in a loud voice that he was going to take the boys to a farming state and remarry. Hope blown asunder. Elene didn't want to talk with us.

The situation wasn't that different, however, from many a time in the past. We assumed Elene was functioning in her own place, even though she couldn't see Karma. Besides, Shirley and I were being wonderfully distracted. I had written a book about my blind years. We had just received those heavenly smelling off-the-press copies and the publishers had already ordered a second printing. These were heady times for us. It was easy to put Elene's problems in a separate compartment and reason she had a roof over her head, was coping pretty well, and maybe Karma would change his attitude. He had before.

But we couldn't hide for long. Within a couple of weeks Elene called from the hospital. She was weeping and frightened. She said she had been brought in because she had been hitting her head with a rock. But they shouldn't have stopped her, because she needed to hit her head with a rock to balance her dental work. My mind caught on her word "balance." That's what she had been seeking for so long.

On the phone she talked incessantly about a man who had a car accident, about a dead cat, about the dissecting of a frog in a high school biology class, about the dangerous wiring in buildings. I listened with occasional "uh-huh's" and felt infinitely sad. The next day she was put on Haldol and Navane.

In the following talks, her voice became thick and hard to understand. She pleaded with us to come up and get her out.

When she was stable again and out, another happy period followed. We went up in August and found her in good shape. Karma had relented and she was seeing the boys again. We bought a nice-looking thrift-shop couch for her Bear Creek house, and since the Buick was so bashed up and too old and unreliable for repair, we bought a used brown Toyota Corolla. It was cheap enough but Elene loved it. The doctor had said she could drive and her license was good. From the used car lot she drove the Corolla up the mountain. I rode with her, heart in throat. Shirley followed behind in our car.

We talked on the way about her medications. They gave her a constantly worried, pained expression, her forehead frowning without her realizing it. There was also some distortion of her face, one side of her mouth drooping. She said she trembled inside. But she admitted that the side effects had subsided in the last few days and she felt confident in driving.

We noted many details of an improved life. She used tampons during her periods, and when we took pictures of the boys, she let us use the flash. Gale and Jonathan stayed with her that night, sleeping on the new couch, and we heard the next morning that Elene first thing had driven down to the market for breakfast cereal and milk. Things were certainly looking up.

All of our phone calls that fall confirmed the improvement. The Bear Creek house worked well. She continued to drive and loved taking the boys to games and special classes, as if she had joined the soccer moms. She told us of volunteering at the homeless soup kitchen, and we reveled in the reversal of roles.

She got a part-time job shelving books in the Boulder Creek public library. When we were next in Santa Cruz we had a chance to meet Mary, the main librarian. She was an older woman who said she had talked a good deal with Elene and had grown to love her. She knew Elene had mental problems, but she discounted them in the light of her unusual intelligence. She thought her analytic perspectives on the economy, the environment, technology, and human relations were sound. As far as Mary was concerned,

Elene's principal problem was overintellectualizing these issues. Mary didn't realize that overintellectualizing was sometimes listed by the psychologists as one symptom of schizophrenia. But what does that mean, and how in the world would anyone test it? When you're dealing with intelligent people, is there such a thing as overintellectualization? Or must we make Einstein schizophrenic?

Elene was nearing forty, and we had been told that some schizophrenics improve during menopause. There was hope. Elene was apparently reconciled to medication. She was coping with a house. She was making a little money on her own. She was helping with the boys, driving them to karate and French lessons. She had survived the wandering-in-the-wilderness years without another pregnancy.

The stable period lasted about six months. On January 21, 1994, Elene called and I noticed her speech pattern had changed. She was once more compulsively rambling, this time about her need to move to a big city. She admitted she had not taken her meds. Under those medications, she wailed, she felt like a whipped slave, and she couldn't go back to them.

Elene's phone calls exposed fears of her present house. She had to move. No insects came inside it. Something was wrong because there were no insects. It had a plastic tub and she couldn't take a shower or a bath in plastic. She had tried to take a shower at Karma's but he didn't want her to do that. I grasped at straws and called Karma, asking if he wouldn't let her take showers there. He said sourly that they would work it out. He clearly resented my interference.

A series of incidents followed like awaited bursts of thunder after lightning. For some time the Children's Protective Services had been visiting them, monitoring conditions at home for a mother who had been so often hospitalized. Now they prohibited Elene from driving the boys. She bemoaned the fact that she could no longer get them to their karate lessons.

Then the landlord sent a bill for new locks since Elene had lost the keys. A week later he sent us an additional bill, this time for an extra tank of propane because he had found that Elene left the heater on day and night whether she was there or not.

Karma called with the awful news that Elene had driven to San Mateo, been caught speeding, was hospitalized there for a few days, and the car was impounded.

The drama was to be played out in southern California, not in her more congenial north. In February we had just gone to bed when Elene called from Cambria. She was driving down to see us, had only two dollars in her pocket, and didn't know where to sleep. A strange man came on the phone and said he wanted to help her, and what did we suggest? We told him to direct Elene to a motel and leave her. Then we told Elene to have the motel call us for a credit card number. But with the phone beside us, no response came the whole night.

Early the next morning a sheriff called to tell us Elene had run out of gas outside Oxnard and we must cover the towing charge. A few hours later the call was from Elene herself. She was in Newport Beach at the corner of San Joaquin Hills and San Miguel roads. That was coincidentally very close to our St. Michaels Church so we knew the area well. We said to wait at the gas station, we would come. When we got there, no Elene. We searched all the parking lots for the brown Toyota, but no Elene.

Assuming she might call again, we went back to our place, and getting off the elevator, we saw Elene in the third floor lounge with two of our women friends. She was dressed somewhat bizarrely in a long, drooping gown and a large garden hat. Somehow I thought of Virginia Woolf.

Elene's hand was wrapped in a bloody towel. She clutched a small paper bag with one organic apple in it and a bottle of sesame oil. Under her arm was a dog-eared copy of Abraham Maslow's *Toward a Psychology of Being*. She had a warm smile for us and we hugged. We asked about her hand, and she said she had cut it on the phone booth door at the gas station. But her voice was frail, subdued, and she seemed more fragile than ever before. Her eyes were glazed and her conversation sadly incoherent. She thought she had spent last night in some grove in Santa Barbara.

In our apartment, we bandaged her hand loosely and Shirley immediately put on some rice to boil. I took Elene to our nearby market to choose the food she wanted to eat. In the produce aisles she actually let me take her hand as she chose vegetables for steaming. Back home, she ate some rice and broccoli and carrots, then fell asleep in a big chair.

By then it was early evening. She did not wake 'til next morning.

After a breakfast of fruit and a small amount of oatmeal, she seemed far less fragile. A retired doctor, Leslie Turlock, lived in a nearby apartment, and we asked him to look at her cut. It was a fairly big gash and was still oozing a bit. He recommended Neosporin right away. Elene bridled. No, wouldn't honey do as well?

"Honey?" said the old doctor. "Honey?" He looked at me and then long at Elene. I could see his mind registering the situation. "Well," he said slowly, "it might work."

So we went back to our apartment and rebandaged the cut with honey.

Elene went out with Shirley to shop for clothes, but no luck. In the afternoon Shirley and I headed for our usual nap. Elene wanted to take a bath, so we set out towels and soap.

When we got up, we found Elene huddled in the tub with about an inch of cold water, unable to get out, she said, because she could not touch the plastic sides. We called a nurse from downstairs to help. Elene's period had just begun and there was blood on the bathroom rug. Shirley got her some tampons and this time she was willing to use them.

My elderly aunt (now ninety-six years old) was living in a retirement community a short walk from ours. Elene had always had a special love for my aunt. I felt that after my mother had died she had transferred her love for my mother to my aunt. Elene's backpack had precious few things for herself, but it did carry a wrapped bar of rose soap as a present. Late the afternoon of the bath, we took Elene over to visit Aunty.

Elene, wearing her long dress and big garden hat, seemed strangely appropriate sitting close to Aunty, bridging three generations. My aunt was pleased with the soap, and the two sat smiling at one another, not saying much. Elene's eyes looking out from under that huge hat were frightening enough, but my aunt seemed to enjoy her. Age and infirmity have an affinity that the rest of us cannot know.

CHAPTER THIRTEEN

That day her outbursts became sporadic, with her voice gradually weakening. She accused us of wanting her to die first so we could have some time to live without her. "If I'm going to die before you," she said, "I have to live fast."

In the early evening I got her a blanket and she curled up on the couch, her Abraham Maslow beside her, and went to sleep. When I tried to get her to bed, she said she couldn't move from the couch because she wanted to go back to Santa Cruz and if she moved she couldn't restore the energy she needed to return. I picked up her Maslow, took it to my desk, and thumbed through the pages. She had marked sentences on love: "a deficit need. It is a hole which has to be filled ... If this healing necessity is not available, severe pathology results." Had we somehow missed providing "the healing necessity"? When? How?

We agreed we had to get her back to Santa Cruz. She was clearly headed for the hospital and rather than be hospitalized here with strangers, it would be far better for her to go where she was known and had been well cared for. We planned to take her north, Shirley driving the Toyota and me following in the Ford. I imagined overcoming fear of freeways by the prospect of always having Shirley leading the way. We hoped to leave the day after next, with one day to get ready.

Elene woke the next morning still on the couch, beginning to spot things with blood, because she was now refusing the tampons. I thought I detected something frantic in Shirley.

After breakfast Elene took a bath and pulled in the mat and rug to protect her from the plastic. She was able to get out with the mat and the rug as props, but she then claimed she couldn't get dressed because Dr. Turlock had done something to her finger that had also caused her clothes not to fit. For an hour or so she ran about with only a towel wrapped around her.

On our two-burner stove, Shirley had fixed artichokes, asparagus, and brown rice flavored with sesame oil from Elene's bottle. Knowing Elene wouldn't want to, Shirley and I planned to go downstairs for a big meal to get stoked up for the trip tomorrow. So we left her eating and listening to music while we went downstairs for a quick dinner.

We were half through when Elene appeared in the dining room, big hat, Maslow, and all. She sat with us a bit, and then when walking back upstairs, she said she had broken something. My heart drubbed. Was it the microwave oven or the TV or the computer, something that symbolized technology?

When we walked in the room there was glass all over the far corner of the room. In the midst of the shards of glass was a heavy Swedish crystal etched with a bear that we bought in England with Elene. Above the mess was another of our English purchases, a large framed etching of Lavenham church, askew with its glass broken and protruding.

As Shirley and I stood in disbelief, Elene kept saying she had to do it because otherwise everyone here would have died. We were too stunned to say much. Suddenly Elene grabbed up her Maslow and backpack and ran out the door and down the hall. We followed, but couldn't find her, not in the laundry room, the lounges, or closets. We looked everywhere to no avail. Shirley, her voice trembling, called the police, reporting the situation.

In time a policewoman arrived with two men, all in plain clothes. After taking information, they were about to begin their search when the phone rang. It was Aunty saying that Elene was there. So what to do now? Of course, we could fetch Elene, but we were becoming frightened. For days she had been resenting us. And here looking at the shards of glass, we saw violence. We worried about spending the night in our small apartment with Elene in such a mood. We asked the policewoman if she would help us get her to a motel for the night. She willingly agreed.

We found Elene with Aunty, watching TV, of all things. The policewoman and her support team stayed in the hall with the door open a crack. Alas, Elene caught sight of them.

She freaked out. "You're going to take me to jail! You're going to commit me!"

We were saying, No, No, No, when the policewoman put her head in the door and said she had no intention of taking her to jail, but only to a motel.

Elene rode with us, the police car following. We kept repeating our weak refrain. We thought she'd be more comfortable in a motel tonight. She could get a good night's sleep before we started back to Santa Cruz in the morning. At the Courtyard motel the room was very nicely furnished with a sparkling bathroom, but to me it seemed as sterile and cold as a tomb. How could I leave her here alone? What would she do? She wouldn't want to watch TV. She had her Maslow to read, but how comforting was that? I was sure we had made a terrible mistake.

Shirley pulled down the covers on the bed, said it was getting late, and we should all try to get some sleep. Elene rejected our hugs and sat upright on the bed. I left her twenty-five dollars for room service. We said good night, closed the door, and thanked the police.

As we drove off, I had trouble explaining even to Shirley how I felt. I had betrayed Elene. This was not the time to abandon her. This was the time to embrace her and hold her close. How could we have done this? How could irrational fears so cloud our thinking? I cursed myself for submitting to fear. Had we embarked on cruelty because of fear? I squeezed close my eyelids and gazed into the loneliness of a strange motel room. Would she ever forgive us for this night? Would we ever forgive ourselves?

Back in our apartment, Shirley and I began cleaning up some of the glass. All that glass, shards and splinters and jagged pieces covering the end of the room. It was Elene's life spread out before us—window after window after window, smashing and crashing, sharp with fury and resentments and fears and tinged with suicidal blood. Let the air in. Let the evil out. Challenge death behind the glass.

A taxi driver called from his car phone with Elene in the backseat. He needed to know directions to our place. Shirley said please take Elene back to the Courtyard.

A bit later we talked with the manager of the Courtyard, a nice woman who reported that Elene was eating a bite in the cafe and she expected she would go back to her room afterward.

Shirley and I went to bed. At one thirty A.M. a call from Elene. She was in a pay phone, frightened, not even knowing where she was. We were baffled. We called the police station and got our woman officer. They would put out an alert for a wandering woman.

A few hours later, Elene called again. This time she knew the street—Barranca. She had walked through the dark streets for nearly four miles, thinking to find our place, but actually walking in the opposite direction. Before we could go further, she said suddenly she saw a police car coming and she hung up.

It wasn't too long before we had a call from our central desk downstairs. It was our old friend Twilla, who said Elene was there. Twilla was an incredibly perceptive and sympathetic woman whom we had known for many years. She seemed to sense the situation and said she would be glad to see that Elene had blankets so she could be comfortable in a quiet corner of the lobby 'til morning. Since it was already four thirty, this seemed sensible. At that point we would probably have taken any suggestion that came along. We had lost control.

We slept a fitful hour or so. We got up to make a few sporadic efforts at packing. Shirley and I looked at each other and suddenly said, "This is ridiculous. We can't do this. We've had practically no sleep. We can't put Shirley alone with Elene in an unkempt Toyota with me driving freeways for four hundred miles when I hadn't driven a freeway for at least thirty years." We weren't thinking very clearly.

We wondered if we could hire someone to drive Elene north. And it was Twilla who came to our rescue. She knew a young woman by the name of Trish who was free that day. We had met Trish, too, and remembered her as a reliable, understanding person. We called her. She was willing if she could take her boyfriend with her. We would pay her $200 and buy them their plane tickets home. By seven thirty the arrangements were completed.

I went downstairs and found Elene on a couch by the window, curled tightly in a fetal position, her big hat at her feet. I tried hard to awaken her, and finally her eyes began to flutter. She started sobbing in the pillow, saying she was so frightened. From under the pillow I pulled her wallet and her copy of Maslow, a hairbrush, a tiny notebook and two boxes of OBs, just about all she had. I put them in a string bag that Shirley had provided. I brushed her hair a bit, picked up her hat and got her to the women's room. I heard the toilet flush within.

I took her to the dining room where we sat far apart from others. Jenny brought us orange juice, oatmeal, toast, and tea. Elene cried hard, talking of death. She said that Gale had once told her that it wasn't death but eternity, and she wondered how she could have boys who were so sweet and who said such wonderful things.

My mind flooded with the tragedy of her being separated from those boys who meant so much to her.

I cried with Elene. She suddenly looked so old to me, with deep lines on her face. My sobs made it hard to talk with the waitress who must have been puzzled by the two of us and was clearly uneasy. By then I was feeding Elene, for she seemed reluctant or incapable of eating, and she took each mouthful like a little child. After the cereal, I poured milk over the bits of toast, and she took those, too.

Trish came with her boyfriend and had me sign a permission statement so they couldn't be charged with kidnapping. Shirley came down with containers of fresh steamed broccoli and brown rice and the last of Elene's things. We walked out to the car with its piles of empty boxes and trash. The boyfriend said something about a bad tire, and my heart stopped at the thought that they might back out. But Trish hugged us and said they would get her there.

Elene sat stoically in back. I suddenly noticed that Trish and her boyfriend both smoked. Dear God, could Elene cope with that?

Shirley and I spent the day limp and worthless, sleeping now and again, trying to keep busy, and jumping whenever the phone rang.

Early that night the call came. Trish described it as a fairly easy day. In the car Elene had slept most of the way, and I could picture her curled in that fetal position, trying to forget the cigarette smoke. But they had made it, and if I knew Elene, she was picking up right where she left, unperturbed by the events of the last few days.

Or so I hoped. Not so for me. I would never forget that night when my fears overcame me and I left her alone in that miserable, lonely, fancy motel room. I know I've done a lot wrong, but that night tops the list. And to think of her wandering through the dark streets of Irvine at three in the morning, walking in the wrong direction, seeking Shirley and me. Can I ever forgive myself for that picture? It was I who had been lost in that night, lost in those footsteps on lonely pavement, even lost, crying, while I fed spoons of oatmeal to a similarly tearful, lost, forty-year-old woman.

In a few days we followed her up to Santa Cruz. It was time for the boys' March birthdays. First we stopped at Elene's house. No one there. The doors and windows were all wide open, and it was a coolish spring day so we closed them and left a note.

We picked up the boys and brought them back to our motel for a swim and a movie and dinner and an overnight bed.

The next morning, still with no word of Elene, we called Wurlitz.

"Sorry you didn't know," he said. "Elene's in the hospital. She was brought there after driving with the car doors open."

We said nothing to the boys, but took them home, and then went to the hospital.

Elene seemed happy to see us. No mention of that ill-fated Irvine night. Had she forgotten it, or just suppressed it for future perusal? Her conversation veered from reality, but in familiar ways. When Elene had to go off to a group session, we talked with Stuart Sermin, the sturdy, soft-spoken man whom we knew well by now. He said he had worked there for eleven years and laughed, "I am growing old with Elene."

This facility and these people were hers when she needed them. We felt warmly justified in our plans to get her back here before letting her be hospitalized in a strange place with strange doctors and strange social workers. In Santa Cruz she had done a lot of wandering, homeless and unaccounted for. But nevertheless she had roots through all those years of unrootedness.

Chapter Fourteen

A Picnic in the Park

We understood that Elene had been hospitalized because she had been driving with the car doors open, but that was hardly the whole story. The doors were open because they had been bashed out by an accident and there was no way they could close. The entire car on the driver's side was crushed. The body shop estimated repairs at over $1,000 and recommended totaling the car.

We had come up to see her, of course, and when we got the details, we went over to the tow yard where the brown Toyota was stored. The car looked indeed to be a candidate for totaling. I rescued from the backseat Elene's big hat, her belt, her battered Abraham Maslow book, and a new knife set that she had bought as a gift for someone, we never knew who.

When we took the items back to Elene, she smiled at the hat and was pleased to get the Maslow. She had missed it and assumed the nurses confiscated it. So now she had back her sociologist, but wherever was he leading her? To a world of simpler societies uncontaminated by smoke alarms and televisions and microwave ovens.

When I asked about the accident, she said it was more important that a dead cat's aura be protected than a few car doors be damaged. Added to so many problems, here was one more burden, for the suffering spirits of dead animals.

We never learned much more about that accident except that the police and the DMV suspended her driver's license indefinitely.

Because she had her Bear Creek house to go to, the hospital discharged her rather soon. Or at least it seemed that way to us, for she did not appear to be much better. We took her back to Bear Creek.

A few weeks later she broke out all the windows of that house. More crashing glass, cool air, sharp, jagged shards of transparency, a mind trying to shatter sorrow. The landlord gave her notice of eviction, and we sadly paid him $200 for the windows. We knew another crisis was looming. Karma wouldn't have her back. She stayed with Oracle in his truck for a while.

Then another man, Freddy Fields, emerged in our phone conversations. He was a friend of Clint Stevens, the "honest but sleazy" man who had driven with us to Berkeley in the rain. Elene described Freddy as a motorcycle rider, and the idea of Elene balancing on the seat behind this young man sent chills through my imagination. But Elene liked his guitar playing, which she described as cleansing. He lived in Brookdale, a wide spot in the redwood groves about five miles below Boulder Creek. He arranged for a cabin for Elene beside his and moved her things from the Bear Creek house. Elene came there directly from another stay in the hospital. The doctor had put her on Risperdal, which he told us had fewer side effects. She recovered unusually quickly and took the move calmly.

Shirley had been diagnosed with cancer and was now undergoing radiation. It consumed our lives. When we thought of Elene, we reasoned that we should be pleased that Freddy Fields seemed to be watching over her, but deep down we knew we were living in a fool's paradise. We suspected that he was as sick as Elene. They were both adopted and each in turn ranted on to us about the importance of finding and knowing their natural mothers. More dangerous, he shared her aversion to medication. One dreary night she admitted to us that she had stopped the Risperdal.

In midsummer Fields called us saying he had missed Elene for a few days until he learned that she was in Dominican. We called Wurlitz and learned that the police had brought her to the hospital when they found her breaking windows with rocks in the little town of Ben Lomond, down the highway from Brookdale.

So here I was again calling up those twin feelings of, first, relief that she was safe in her familiar hospital and, second, guilt that I should be doing more than I was. When we talked with Elene, her voice was thick and she was having cramps, but she had started Risperdal again, this time with Cogentin. She was pleased that Freddy Fields had brought her some special snacks. Shirley sent her some flowers, simple ones, daisies, the kind she loved.

On the phone in a few days she seemed much better. The cramps had subsided. That day she was discharged. She called a few days later, excited at having seen Gale on the mall with Karma. Gale had hugged her and seemed glad to see her, but then had gone off to a bench to read. She said he was so engrossed in his reading. She did not know what the book was.

I called Gale and learned he was deep into Tolkien's *Lord of the Rings*. There was a time when Elene had been absorbed with Tolkien, and Shirley and I had followed her through the hobbits' adventures. Now it was Gale escaping from this messy world—his world of a missing mother—while his mind struggled instead with little Frodo to find the fires of Mordor where he could liberate mankind from the ring of evil.

We tried to picture Elene in her Brookdale cabin in the redwoods with Freddy Fields living nearby. One day I called her and a strange man's voice answered.

"I'm Charles Blastin. I'm taking care of Elene. I've been living with her for the last nine days."

"Does she need taking care of?"

"Yeah. In a way. She's smart enough not to take those poisons they give her. But I've tried to get her to two appointments with her doctor and she won't go."

"Can I talk with Elene?"

There was a pause and then he came back on the line. "She doesn't want to talk with you."

What could I say? I flustered around with things like "Please take care of her," and "Call me if anything changes," and "I'll call you tomorrow."

The next day it was Freddy Fields who called. He said that Elene wanted to get rid of Blastin and he was trying to help her do it but it wasn't easy. I asked to talk with Elene and this time she came. For what seemed to me an hour she rambled on about the horrors of medications and hospitals, about the impossibility of getting to doctors' appointments or court hearings, and I couldn't get her to comment on Fields or Blastin. Shirley and I decided we had to go up.

Shirley had bounced back from her radiation therapy and the pain in her legs was almost gone. We flew up and rented a car, and it seemed that getting on that familiar trail was an additional boost to Shirley—back to see her ailing daughter and maybe find some way to help.

It was our first visit to the Brookdale cabin. It stood with a few other cabins on a high foundation in the midst of magnificent redwoods. The air was so sweet. No answer to our knock. We pushed open the unlocked door and entered a familiar shambles. The one room was dark, its few pieces of furniture dismantled. A card table slanted on three legs. Clothes and wrinkled paper bags, dirty cups and plates were thick on the floor. The little kitchen was a jumble of unwashed pots and decaying food. The refrigerator was only half cold and the freezer had water in the bottom. The sink was cracked and half falling from the wall.

We swallowed deep, closed the door, and found Elene at Freddy Fields' place two redwood trees away. We put Elene in the car, picked up some picnic things, collected the boys, and planned a Santa Cruz picnic and afternoon in the park, a nice dinner, and a stay in our motel for the night.

We started down the mountain with Shirley driving, Elene and the two boys in the backseat. Jonathan and Gale started arguing and tussling. I told them to calm down. That incensed Elene. She started screaming at us, louder and louder. Shirley and I suddenly became like dragons to her. If the boys had problems, we had caused them because we let them drink sugared sodas in motels in front of TV. She was talking fast now: Shirley should do something about her "big titties," and she could do something because they had been caused by the bridge in her mouth.

Without a pause she started at me. I should stop using my height to lord over people. There were some wild references to machetes. It was clear she was losing control.

Shirley was shaking. She said she couldn't drive any farther. By then we were down the mountain. I said, just get us to Mark Stevens Park, not far away.

It was Monday and the park was nearly empty. Shirley, shaking with tears, left the car immediately, walked off a distance, and sat alone at a wooden picnic table. Elene got out on her side and walked off in the other direction, talking constantly.

I took from the trunk the box of picnic food, told the boys to come when they were through arguing, and went to a third table nowhere near the others.

Jonathan was the first to come. I got him a root beer from the picnic bag, and then a fear shot through me that Elene would come back, see him drinking a soda, and start in all over again. So I said, "Finish it up." He didn't, and wanted to save the rest. I said no and threw the can in the trash barrel. He ran off crying, so I retrieved the can from the barrel and took it to him. Tell me I shouldn't have done it! Tell me I was spoiling him! But at that point I would have done most anything to gain peace.

Sometimes a little time can relieve, if not heal. Shirley, the boys, and I gradually assembled for a half-hearted lunch. And an hour or so later all of us, including Elene, climbed back into the car and decided we'd like a walk by the ocean. So with the boys pretty silent and Elene still jabbering, we drove to Moss Landing on Monterey Bay and walked on the dunes by the sea. The surf and the sea wind seemed to pound us together like shingled pebbles, though Matthew Arnold's eternal note of sadness was not far off.

We ended in town at a taco place. Right away Elene disappeared and we saw her walking across the street to a mom-and-pop store from which she came back with a gift for Shirley and me of Carr's Water Crackers. She remembered that we liked them in England. As gifts go, that was gold and myrrh and frankincense all wrapped into a package of water crackers.

Elene didn't eat anything because she said she was fasting. She wrapped up her share of tortillas and suddenly got up and went outside. We watched her through the windows. She walked back and forth 'til a homeless woman came by in long, ragged dress pushing a cart. Elene gave the tortillas to the woman and returned to us.

She wanted to go back to her Brookdale cabin for the night. When we got to the cabin, she told us she lived in a closet so the whole world had to be her living room. There was some truth there. She had become like a perpetually homeless person, at least homeless in spirit. For her the whole world was her living room and she wandered through it with a mix of love and worry and compassion and fear.

When we picked her up the next day, we felt again her clutching at reeds of hope. This time it was reference books that she needed. She said she wanted "tedium and boredom," and reference books would help. I wondered if they really meant stability to her, and who could argue that her life could stand some of that?

In the months that followed Shirley and I went about our daily routines, praying to ourselves that Shirley's cancer would remain quiescent just as we hoped that Elene's illness would not erupt into some new tragic form. We were getting frequent, long, bizarre phone calls from Elene. Reference books became one of the recurrent themes. If I had any inkling that they would help, I would have sent her my whole shelves of Bartlett and Webster and Collier's, all my world almanacs, atlases, and encyclopedias—each of which she probably remembered from my bookcases as she was growing up.

But reference books were not her sole anxieties. She never gave up on her desire to live elsewhere in the world in some simpler culture. Also her fears of locked facilities and of death emerged quite often. She worried still that all the people around her who smoked were contaminating the earth and their own lives. And she feared she was charged with too much electricity, probably from the wiring in buildings. Her sense of smell was all off, though she was sure that had to do with the tapping of Micah's spine in the hospital.

There was a dramatic new concern—that she was not mentally ill but mentally retarded. I could only think of her wonderful mind and her artistic accomplishments. Now she rambled on about how she needed to live only among mentally retarded people.

Shirley and I ... ...pare notes from these conversations, and we compiled ... ...ble vignettes of Elene's
life. She ... street ... ... in the Big Sur,
giving ... ... down a street
when a ... ... bloody victim,
...her ... es. Or again she
told of ... ... a dead cat on the
... Once she buried a
... green eggs on the
... natural," she said,
... among the orange

...ltuous. Shirley and I
... how lonely our child,
...lations was talking often
... situation. And we once
...iance for the Mentally Ill
... supported for years.

...eling when a call came from
...ken all the windows in her
...last seen her walking down the
...aid he would go up and find her
...

...en, I should have saved it for five
...came from Elene. She was in tears
...d, "What am I going to do?" Through
..."Ask Papa if he wouldn't mind if you
didn... ... The call came from the hospital where
Wurlitz had ta... ... he found her in the rain. She had been
there five days and du...g that time the doctors had told her she
was pregnant. They had taken her off all medications. She thought
the father was Charles Blastin but she really couldn't remember
much about that period. All I could think of was rape.

When she told Karma, he was furious and said he would sue
for divorce. Elene refused to talk about abortion. She was sure
that the baby had been waiting for birth and it would be wrong
to block its coming. She admitted she couldn't care for the child

herself because she felt she was mentally retarded. Maybe, she cried, she could find a religious group or a family that would take her in and help her raise the baby.

Wurlitz told us the agencies must and would now assume full protection for both mother and child. They will probably keep her hospitalized for the whole pregnancy. There are now two to safeguard. On birth, he predicted, the Children's Protective Services would take custody and place the baby immediately in foster care. He sighed that he had one client who had had ten children, the last eight of whom had been removed at birth.

That night, to get our minds off the problems, we went nearby to a piano recital by two young women. During the Liszt and Chopin, I could think of nothing but Elene. How like them she could have been—gifted, musically talented, imaginative. And now she was in a locked facility, pregnant by a strange man, estranged from her husband and boys, convinced that she was mentally retarded, which she wasn't. Through Chopin's teardrop Prelude I could hear Elene cry.

Chapter Fifteen

Trinity, the Mighty Morphin

In November 1994 Elene was sent to Crestwood, a long-term locked facility in San Jose that specialized in the pregnant mentally ill. At first she hated it. She couldn't get away from the smell of people who smoked and the food was too buttery. There was no library or piano.

Gradually the phone calls got better. She liked one of her three roommates. And Crestwood, like most of these facilities, worked with a system of patient credits—points for attending group meetings, for helping in the work, for good grooming—and Elene soon earned enough credits to take an excursion with a nurse. They walked to a Christmas tree lot down the street, and she told us how she loved the smell and the feel of the fir branches.

Elene was talking to Shirley from Crestwood. She felt nothing was easy for her. "There seem to be a hundred pieces in the puzzle and I have only fifteen." Then she told Shirley she loved her, and somehow that hurt even more than when she screamed. She asked Shirley to help her make her space in the locked facility more her own with pictures and little things.

We flirted for a while with the prospect of a private facility for the pregnancy, and we proposed a few to Elene (even The Farm in Tennessee, which traditionally had taken pregnant women into its commune), but none seemed to appeal.

After Elene bit a nurse, the doctors put her on Prolixin and Cogentin, which they considered the safest combination for the baby. There were, as usual, severe side effects. She couldn't sit for more than a minute or two, and she couldn't read or concentrate. Her speech became badly slurred, and she cried, "What if the baby can't talk?"

We went up in December. The first view of Crestwood, even on a cold, rainy day, was not bad. It was set in a marginal neighborhood of gas stations and small stores with blazing signs. But the building was low, modern, and imaginative with a flagstone facade, semihidden among trees. The outer rooms, for visitors only, were carpeted and nicely furnished, but beyond the double layer of locked doors it was traditional hospital—vinyl floors, long unfurnished corridors, fluorescent lighting—details that had come to spell loneliness to me.

The head nurse brought Elene. We hugged. I thought I detected a little bulge in her belly. Elene seemed proud that she had earned enough credits to be checked out for a few hours. We said we had noticed a Swedish massage shop nearby and offered her one. I had not forgotten the polarity days. Fortunately when we got there, they could take her in and we left her for an hour. That was a big success. Afterward we had lunch at a German delicatessen.

When we came back to Crestwood, I asked if it felt like coming home, and she only smiled. We went through the locked doors to see her to her room. Patients stood in a long line getting medications, and one man was yelling at the top of a wild, booming voice, "Motherfuckers, fucking Jews, niggers." I cringed for Shirley and it even bothered me. But Elene marched along, paying no attention. Her hall was relatively peaceful.

The hospital Christmas tree was big and pretty enough, but its branches offered invisible shadows and unreachable coldness.

The next day, we picked her up in the early afternoon, did a little Christmas shopping, and went to Karma's where the boys were. We decorated their Christmas tree and wrapped presents. We went out for tacos. It all worked fine except that Gale threw up his tacos.

At Crestwood Elene became a model patient. Everybody loved her. She got the highest points of any other patient week after week. She went with a group to a movie (*Forrest Gump*), for a swim at a local YMCA, and for a dance class. It seemed clearer and clearer that she was not right for Crestwood, and Wurlitz and her conservator devised a plan to have her moved back to SART.

Of course, that was not what Elene wanted. She wanted to get out completely, to find a family to live with through the birth. She conceived plan after plan. She answered an ad in the paper from a woman named Lynn who on the phone said she would take Elene. She offered to pick up Elene on an overnight pass to show her place. Lynn had three children of her own and lived with two other "guests." Elene wisely sensed there would be endless tensions if she and a baby were added to that household. Still, she was ready to try it. Wurlitz turned it down cold.

Then Elene became excited about open adoptions. In such arrangements the biological mother becomes a frequent visitor and helper in raising the child. She babysits, for example, assists when the child is ill, and joins in family festivities like birthdays or Thanksgivings. The prospect fitted neatly into Elene's ideals for extended families, and it wasn't a ridiculous hope, for some measure of such openness was occasionally available in adoptions. But the county adoptive agencies weren't into such arrangements, and they were the ones who now called the shots.

It was rather late when the baby's natural father surfaced. Elene surprised us when she said that Charles Blastin had visited her several times at Crestwood, and they had talked about living together. The idea didn't seem too exciting to Elene, but we could tell she was getting desperate for any way to get out. Wurlitz told us that Blastin's father was a well-placed physician in Santa Cruz, and my mind jumped at the prospect of his taking responsibility for the deeds of his son. But what did we know of that son as a husband?

Shirley was instinctively repulsed by the idea of Blastin entering the picture again, but I weakly revived my argument on the importance of a father and a name, and in this case especially if there were a wealthy physician in the background. But Elene told us she didn't want to marry Blastin. She held to the belief that Karma would come around. She said she still loved Karma, and some way would be found for her to keep this baby.

The months went by and one after another of her hopes dimmed. When the county adoption agency reported to her that

CHAPTER FIFTEEN

they had found an ideal family for adoption, Elene called us, sobbing, saying she couldn't give up this child. She would rather die.

When we went up in February, Elene had been moved from SART to a transitional house (T-house) on Prather Lane. The doctors had decided she was doing well enough to be allowed more independence as long as she was also supervised.

We found the T-house on a sidestreet in a rural area without curbs or paved sidewalks. It was a sprawling one-story stucco with no front yard but grass and trees in back. The living room had vinyl sofas and a television, and around the edge of the dining room were a few shelves of books and small tables holding patients' projects—beads, ceramics, or stamps.

Elene shared a room with another woman. In it were a small cupboard that held her clothes and a headboard over her single bed with two or three books (including Abraham Maslow), some art postcards we had sent her, and a vase she had made at Crestwood. There were ten patients in the house and a supervisor who had a room near the entrance from which she oversaw medications, group meetings, chores, comings and goings.

Elene showed us around T-house. She introduced us to Joe and Maxine, both of whom wandered off into the backyard. We suggested that she get an overnight pass, and that she and the boys could then spend the night with us in the motel. She seemed pleased at the idea, but said she hoped we could have a conference with Wurlitz, that she needed to talk with him about her plans, and our being there might make him more sympathetic.

When we called him at his office it was late in the afternoon but he said to come right over. After pleasantries, we said we looked forward to having Elene together with the boys tonight, and then Elene began with a request that she be allowed to take a yoga class. But she quickly went on to wondering what would happen if her parents were willing to rent her a house. Then she moved into her familiar plea to find some way to be involved with raising the child. She had no new proposals, but this time simply threw herself on him, asking for some help.

As Elene talked, Wurlitz frowned and looked from her to the parking lot outside his window. Finally he interrupted her.

"Look, Elene, I know what you're saying. I know only too well what you want, but you have to listen to me."

He proceeded to be relentlessly firm. She could not stay with us at the motel overnight. She could not take a yoga class unless she got permission from prenatal care and even then could not travel on a public bus. He then added something that indicated how close he was to events in her life. He told her that under no conditions was she again to see Charles Blastin. Moreover, he said it was much too early to think of renting a house. He might be able to arrange for a slightly more independent situation, but then came his clincher. He saw no chance of her keeping the baby.

Elene sat stoically, not breaking down, but staring at him with watery eyes. She said nothing more. It was as if she had been through this so many times that only weariness remained.

He apologized for his brusqueness, said it had been a long day. We mumbled our thanks and good-byes and walked down the hall on either side of Elene. I wanted so badly to put my arms around her, but I sensed it would be a mistake.

We knew she liked an Indian restaurant called Malabar and when we suggested it, she nodded absentmindedly. In the restaurant she ate little, but now and again unexpectedly she would simply cry.

The next day we took Elene and the boys to the park and they played Frisbee. When they rested on the bench, she encouraged the boys to talk about the baby, even listening at her belly. Jonathan had a new toy, a talking sword, and he held it tight to Elene's stomach and turned it on. The machine belted out, "Tigersword Power Now." He repeated it over and over. "Those will be the baby's first words," Jonathan assured us seriously. And he went on to give Elene a name for the baby. "We have to name her for one of the Mighty Morphin Power Rangers. If it's a girl, she'll have to be Trini."

Elene frowned. "It seems incomplete."

"How about Trinity then?"

Elene smiled. "I like Trinity."

To keep Elene happy, Wurlitz arranged for satellite housing with a shade more independence than at the T-house, but with a minimum of supervision. It was a cluster of four or five small three-bedroom cottages, recently built behind a row of commercial stores on Water Street. Once behind the stores, the area opened with trees and small gardens. Elene was assigned a corner room with its own entrance plus kitchen and living room privileges.

She now hoped that she could fix the room so nicely that the agencies would change their minds and let her bring the baby there, at least for a while. Unknown to us, she had saved literally everything from Gale and Jonathan's baby days, even a carrying cradle, and had stashed them away in back closets at Karma's. Now she inveigled Karma to put together some shelves for one wall and to bring the baby things. She arranged them neatly in stacks on the shelves.

The baby was due in May. This was April, and now we learned that T. S. Eliot was correct—April is the cruelest month. Shirley had been diagnosed with a primary cancer and it was pancreatic, one of the worst. And as we wrestled with this grim word, Elene, knowing nothing of Shirley's diagnosis, began to seem further and further off center. Once on the phone she didn't know whether it was morning or night. Mary Moss, who was now acting as her midwife, called us to express her worries.

Toward the end of April Wurlitz informed us she had been remanded once more to the hospital. He said she was probably not eating because she looked gaunt. Either she had stopped taking her medications or they had failed to work. Clearly the extra degree of independence had been a terrible mistake.

He and we all felt relieved that she was back in the security of the mental health unit. Those thoughtful people made it possible for her midwife to visit her day or night. At delivery time the midwife would be with her in the hospital's birthing center. Shirley and I, distracted by our own news, blessed Santa Cruz once more for taking thoughtful charge.

On May 2, 1995, the news came early in the morning. The baby had been born. Shirley gathered her strength, and we got on a plane that afternoon, arriving in Santa Cruz about seven thirty in the evening. We went straight to the hospital and to the maternity ward. Elene was not there. We were surprised. She had been returned right after the birth to the mental health unit. A nurse insisted that we come in to see the baby. She put Shirley in a wooden rocking chair and brought over a beautiful little girl whom she called Trinity. The nurse brought a bottle and let Shirley feed her. She seemed a perfect newborn—no wrinkles, no redness, a small shock of blonde hair. Watching her face, screwing up her nose, we were convinced of her burgeoning personality. As Shirley rocked, I thought I heard Mozart on the hospital's Muzak.

When we got to Elene, she was upset that she had been forced back to the mental health unit so fast without even a post-partum night with the baby. The immediate separation encapsulated the larger grief. She looked a little tired, but not terribly so. No one would ever guess that she had given birth early that morning, and we remembered other birth days in which she had cleaned the house or picked up Chinese food on the way home. We talked 'til well after nine when we were far more exhausted than the new mother.

The next morning we went back to the nursery so Shirley could rock and feed Trinity once more. The foster parents were coming to take her at three that afternoon. While we were there, midwife Mary Moss came, held Trinity, and we could see Mary's tears fall on Trinity's blanket. When we parted, Mary promised to see that Elene had all the right teas and herbs for healing.

Elene seemed physically strong that day. She had kept the nightgown in which she had given birth, and all that first night had held it close so she could smell the baby. She still hoped to see Trinity again, feeling comforted that the child was at least in a building close by. By then it was afternoon, and we did not tell her that the foster parents had already come and gone, and Trinity was with them.

What would the next steps be for Elene? Where would she go when the hospital dismissed her now? We wanted to keep up Elene's spirits, but the picture seemed so bleak. We were relieved when Wurlitz and Stuart Sermin came in and said they were glad to see us all together. They wanted to talk about the future.

They started out with proposals of psychotherapy, but Elene countered softly. Words had never helped her that much, she said.

Stuart suggested that maybe art therapy would be nice, and he said he had seen such beautiful sand trays. Brother, I thought, he's really reaching for it. Sand trays to assuage a mother's grief for a lost child! I don't know why I thought of Rachel in the Bible, crying for her lost children. How long had Rachel cried? Surely no one had offered her sand trays.

Wurlitz reported that Charles Blastin had been calling but he had not been told about the baby. Elene said she could not be sure he was the father. He was certainly there, but she did not remember those days at all. Wurlitz and Sermin both recommended that for paternity on the birth certificate Elene should put "unknown." Then if there were an adoption, only Elene and Karma would need to consent.

I thought that was a cruel subject, too, but everything seemed cruel to me at that point. It was a bit gentler when they suggested that Elene might wish to spend a period again at T-house but also keep her room on Water Street, which she could continue to fix up. Sure, I thought, but what's the incentive now?

Visiting that night, bringing the biggest bunch of gerbera daisies we could buy, we found Elene alert but subdued. Her eyes looked as if a huge storm had passed through her, leaving weather-beaten quietness and water dripping. The past was distantly thundering, its sorrow having pounded against an amazing inner strength.

She knew now that Trinity was gone. Elene had been told that the foster parents had previously adopted a boy who had a schizophrenic mother. They were hoping to find a baby girl to be his sister, and Trinity was ideal for them. For Elene there was no more talk of open adoption, of babysitting, of tending her child when sick, of birthday parties, of Thanksgiving dinners.

We left her staring at the daisies with the wisp of a smile, the unmelting kind of a smile that is not based on joy.

Driving back to the motel, Shirley was planning tomorrow. "We'll bring the boys to see her. She needs that."

I said, "Sure." But I was looking at Shirley and thinking, My God, I know now where Elene got her inner strength. This woman sitting beside me has gone beyond the sadness of watching a beautiful little granddaughter whisked away from her just as she was rocking and feeding her. I could see Shirley in that rocking chair bonding with a baby in her arms, a child she was about to lose to the generations of the adopted. I saw her watch Mary Moss crying without breaking down herself. How could she not be thinking of her own sentence of pancreatic cancer? How could the cabin of her brain contain such thoughts without tears? Was she declaring that death could not harm her more than knowing her child cried to nurse her newborn baby, our lost Trinity?

The images of those two women on that day in May will live on with me forever as the sweetest and bitterest of memories. I never feel the bitterness without also realizing the bravery of those two women, unbelievable tenacity in the face of loss. I have read so many novels of strong women. I remember Hester Prynne bearing her exile from society. I remember Scarlett O'Hara, scraping the burnt earth. I remember Dorothea Casaubon, stronger than her husband, and the same with Irene Forsyte, resolute before the man of property. I remember Alexandra Bergson triumphant over a frontier environment. I remember Clarissa Dalloway, struggling to bring together the floating parts of her mind. Vocally or quietly these fictional women faced incursive societies, crushing human relations, and cruel environments. But I also knew and could embrace in my own arms two women who embodied the fortitude of them all.

Shirley died early the following year. The doctors had offered her radiation, chemotherapy, or surgery, but they had admitted none of these would extend life more than a half year. Shirley turned them all down in favor of a few months of peaceful decline. In the end she never had to leave our apartment, surrounded by the spinet piano (which she played almost to the end), our books, and our pictures.

During those last six months, there were many good days. As she played Mozart or worked at her computer, she inevitably thought about the past. In bed at night we would talk about our life with Elene and I began to realize how much Shirley remembered that I had forgotten, especially about the early years. She encouraged me to write things down, and every morning

I recorded what she told me the night before. We would then talk over the draft and revise it. We got more and more involved; we spent hours and hours on the project. Shirley even pored over old financial records to give us dates and recall events. I had kept journals much of the time, and we elaborated on those. It became a joint enterprise that helped ease the pain of what we knew was coming.

It seemed to please Shirley that we could reconstruct so completely our joys and fears, that we could so capture and review our lives before she said farewell. Those pages are the heart of this book. Though here my emotions predominate because they are the best known to me, it was Shirley who made it all possible.

A few weeks before the end, Elene and Karma and the boys came down to visit. Though Shirley was then confined to bed, the boys at ten and twelve were blithely unaware of the coming tragedy. They were far more interested in Disneyland. But it was a joy for Shirley to see Elene and Karma together again, knowing that they all now lived at the old house in Boulder Creek. Shirley could die seeing for the time some healing balm was working in the world.

Chapter Sixteen

Thoughts at Daybreak

It is now eight years since Shirley died. I live in the same apartment and sleep in the same bed we used. I never drift off at night without telling Shirley I love her and miss her. I'm told that's all right as long as she doesn't talk back. I speak with Elene by phone several times a week. Though Shirley remains silent, Elene talks back remarkably and seems blessedly normal.

Elene is now on a medication called Zyprexa, which with a minimum of side effects, has given her a new lease on stability. Sometimes the doctors combine Zyprexa with other drugs like Risperdal, which for her causes vivid dreams. She says they're not nightmares, just eidetic images. Recently she dreamed of being housed in a community of ancient prehistoric dwellings as at Mesa Verde or the Acoma pueblo. But she wasn't happy living there, and I wondered if she had resolved her old desire to find a primitive society that would conform to her nontechnological aspirations.

Trinity, like Micah, is now legally adopted. A court had to finally free the baby for adoption. Karma had assented, but Elene could never bring herself to sign the papers.

She has left Water Street with its shelves of baby clothes and now assigned to a room in a county satellite house with seven others. The room is nicely decorated with books, hangings, and teapots. She spends two-thirds of her time there. Otherwise she's at Boulder Creek, cooking, laundering, and cleaning for Karma and the boys. If the tensions become too great, she can retreat to the satellite house. The constancy and continuity of the situation plus the medication have created a picture that is more hopeful than at any time since we took her to Santa Cruz over forty years ago.

Gale at twenty-one works in a coffee shop, attends community college, and hopes to be a graphic designer, using computers. Jonathan is also in community college, loving modern music and dance but planning to become a criminal lawyer. He and Elene often go to events together since they share a fascination with music and dance. When I hear of Jonathan taking Elene to dinner and a concert, happily often, my heart sings.

Has Elene recovered from her illness? Who can tell? Sometimes I am told the condition simply burns itself out. One-quarter of schizophrenics are seen as cured, at least to the point of becoming functioning members of society. There is one theory that women schizophrenics do much better after menopause. Glory be, if that is true. But also glory be to Zyprexa. Glory be to the Santa Cruz mental health people. And above all, glory be to Elene—Elene the fair, Elene the lovable, the lily maid of Santa Cruz whose face may not have launched a thousand ships, but whose life has certainly led at least two of us from the heights to the depths and back to the heights again.

During Shirley's last months we thought a lot about Elene, her life and ours. Was the fundamental badge of her illness the fact that she could not stick to the simple business of living? Uncomplicated straightforwardness—putting one foot in front of the other without thinking, eating whatever comes, taking work orders without too much questioning—can be satisfying, even sufficient, for most people. Charlie Chaplin munching shoelaces in *The Gold Rush* isn't asking about the ecological implications of plastic or leather. A long time ago Oliver Wendell Holmes called insanity "the logic of an accurate mind overasked." Elene has "overasked" herself.

For Elene the broader themes intrude and obsess. She sees beyond surface reality into deeper meanings. The modern philosopher-monk Thomas Moore wonders if some forms of mental illness might be "a relief from the stringent limits of pragmatic, sanitized life. It is a door that opens out from human reason to divine mystery." It requires us to be cured of our "anemic imagination." Elene's imagination is anything but anemic. When she sees microwave ovens, they emit waves of dreadful consequence. The glass on the picture in our living room was somehow connected with death, and she had to break it to release us. Words accumulate special meanings, and a simple phrase like "good night" can assume threatening proportions. It is a hyperactive awareness, an attachment to symbols, a world of tokens and epiphanies that does not test well with reality as defined by most of us who experience it.

Elene's cosmology leads to high and confident expectations, which may or may not have anything to do with her illness. Her preference for walking is part of a larger craving for, even an unquestioning commitment to, a primitive, nontechnological society. The simple walking part is an acceptable and manageable program in her life, but her expanded vision collides with a society traveling in a different direction.

She searches for a rural way of life based on face-to-face communities, extended families, and handiwork, yet she maintains an attachment to urban pleasures like the classical arts, the piano, the ballet, and the theater. Hence comes the thrashing ambivalence—the vacillation between the dreams of a Hutterite commune on a border frontier and the clanging bustle of urban San Francisco.

Of course, the rest of us dream beyond our capacities and require no consistency in our dreams. Thomas Moore suggests that polytheism—a number of gods—once made it more possible to live with multiplicity, with "the competing demands of the soul." Perhaps Elene would have lived more successfully in such an environment—in ancient Greece, perhaps—for surely in her present situation the gaps between the competing demands of her soul set up tensions which have emotionally and mentally tested her endurance. Those tensions stem from what is more likely related to her illness—the inability to make decisions, and not only on the big issues of her life but on the day-to-day questions of clothing, food, and activity. Her overactive intellect sees endless possibilities and a driving need to review each one with pros and cons under searchlights of doubt.

Delusions have been plentiful, and we were long struck at the persistence of glass among them. How many panes she broke, how many fingers bleeding of glass cuts. Andrew Solomon in his book on depression tells of "a glass delusion" in which some mentally ill people believe themselves made of glass, even resisting human embraces or fearing to sit down because of their glass buttocks. With Elene glass seemed more of a threat, bulging out in earthquakes, barricading against fresh air or freedom, even embracing death itself.

She once expressed to me her frustration at having ideas that exceed her practical abilities. At that point she was thinking of a restaurant that dealt only in the color green—a dining area decorated in green, many living plants, menus that offered asparagus or spinach soup, manicotti with artichokes, salads and sprouts, drinks with green melon, and green-tea ice cream. But, she sighed, "I can't even take care of the receipts. I tell others, and only others can make my dreams happen."

Yet just as she thinks in grand or global terms, she has remained maddeningly self-absorbed, even narcissistic. The original Greek Narcissus was not in love with himself but with his reflection in the pool, which he did not recognize as himself, and the story ends with his transformation into the most beautiful of flowers, a daffodil. I like to think of that when I read that narcissism in its narrowest form is said to be typical of schizophrenics, a symptom of the illness. Looked at as a symptom, it was easy to understand and forgive. After Elene knew of Shirley's cancer, there were many phone calls in which her own problems blocked out even asking how Shirley was. We reasoned that such forgetfulness was not so much self-absorption as the response of a person who was metaphorically suspended by her fingertips, needing all available self-concentration just to hang on over the reflecting pool.

We consequently never expected Christmas presents or Mother's Day cards. They came, but only occasionally. We knew she would have the thought and then would suffer biting frustration at no action. Witness the card at the time of Shirley's hip surgery, written, not sent, received by us three years later. What went on in Elene's mind when she came across the unsent card? How many similar notes were written but never found again? She asked once if I would like to know the presents she had wanted to buy for me but didn't have the money or the courage to get.

But mostly we felt disengagement in her response to the world, a feeling that the proper time for presents or calls or meetings may or may not come, but there is little reason to hurry the moment or try to influence its coming.

Often Elene's concentration on her own problems was evident in her rambling talk, babbling on and on. Babbling may be an unkind word in this situation, for it suggests persons who simply like the sound of their own voice. For Elene that pattern of speech was more likely a reflection of her illness. It was as if her mind was being flooded with sensations, bombarded with images. And some of these cascaded out of her own past, remembering childhood events lost to Shirley and me. That is not to say that we could not fathom her meanings, but even with careful attention, it was hard. The barriers are high in these settings, and I noticed that others in talking with Elene would give up, say "uh-huh," and try to escape. I remember when she went on and on about being made "less energy efficient" because her baby had been injected with antibiotics. And the conclusion was, "If I ate a chicken I'd eat the whole thing and put the feathers on my coat." I'm sure others took the talk as meaningless, but I could see how it only skipped a few transitions. She was reflecting her ecological concerns—energy conservation, the overuse of antibiotics, and wasteful consumption. But the connections were missing. At other times the connections were there but they stemmed from arcane ideas like auras. Sometimes they mirrored a general defiance of established rules. Disordered as they seemed, in her mind they made perfect sense.

There are those who have romanticized mental illness. The psychoanalyst Thomas Szasz called schizophrenia a "fake disease," no more than a semantic fiction. Thomas Moore comes at it from another direction, making the prevailing society mad and proposing a new syndrome in the psychologist's arsenal, one that includes "blind faith in technology, inordinate attachment to material gadgets and conveniences, uncritical acceptance of the march of scientific progress, devotion to the electronic media, and a life-style dictated by advertising." In other words, Elene's mind is less ill than the society's at large. Such thinking was especially evident during the 1960s, interestingly enough, the period in which Elene matured. R. D. Laing, for example, the Scottish psychological researcher and cult figure, thought of schizophrenia not as a breakdown, but as a breakthrough, "a potential liberation and renewal as well as enslavement and existential death." Causative blame rested primarily on a maddening world and a sick society. And schizophrenia was "a special strategy that a person invents in order to live in an unlivable situation." It is certainly true that Elene found the wider world with its technology a threatening place, terribly so, even at times overwhelming. And if I stretch my mind enough, I could say she had invented a strategy to live in an "unlivable situation." Still I'm glad that Laing also recognized "enslavement."

Certainly when Elene was ill, the technological machines of the world took on threatening proportions; they seemed to be inhabited with what some societies would call ghosts or spirits. Transport these earlier societies to today, as Elene would do, and they might well imagine that the practice of modern medicine can call forth genies that perform evil operations on unsuspecting patients in the night. Primitive societies might easily see a spirit in microwave ovens or televisions and be sure the spirit was pouring out destruction. The natives in the movie *The Gods Must Be Crazy* did it to a Coke bottle. They would undoubtedly have seen the ghost of the smoke alarm as a far more frightful force. The psychologist Carl Jung hypothesized that modern man, denying explanations that go beyond his material world, has thereby lost his sense of the soul, for it is the soul that transcends our physical bodies or objects. If the soul comprises the "myths, rituals and poetry" of our inner lives (as Thomas Moore says), it seems that Elene is unwittingly projecting concepts that point to that kind of soul. Has she in a roundabout way found her soul again? In this context, is it too wild to remember that Mary Magdalene, a woman who had once been "possessed of spirits" (was it schizophrenia?) was the first one to see and hear the risen Jesus?

But Elene is not living in a society that generally sees spirits inhabiting natural objects, and when she does see them, when (or if) she is ill, she must feel cut off, divided, estranged, and metaphorically lost in a smoke-filled room. This estrangement, as it does with many schizoids, invites a rejection of conventional ways and leads to unusual dress, dropping out, and antagonistic alienation.

Perhaps the amazing thing is that she ultimately grapples with the fears. Some of her strength could come straight from her ecologically sound lifestyle, eating vegetarian and organic, even freeing her conscience by recycling every possible can or bottle or paper. Massage and tai chi and polarity have relaxed her. Dance and the arts have offered creative outlets. Without these aids, she may well have been hospitalized more often and recovered more slowly.

Would Elene have done better if she had early learned to accept her medications? I would like to think that is true, but I am not at all sure of it. There is good reason to believe that those early psychotic drugs like Haldol and Navane would in the long term have done her more harm than good. The novelist Jay Neugeboren certainly thought so in his memoir about his schizophrenic brother, *Imagining Robert*. He felt that the madness in throwing a bunch of drugs at somebody and hoping they would work in the end deprived his brother of no less than his humanity. If Elene's brain could be compared to Swiss cheese—primarily sound and intact but with occasional holes of vulnerability—it is not impossible that the drugs simply added more holes. Shirley and I felt that each time Elene left the hospital after prolonged medication she seemed less robust, less competent, diminished in capacity. Some of that might have been simply growing older, some from more experience with life, some from constantly facing sobering difficulties. But some could also have been the debilitating effect of psychotic drugs.

Nevertheless, we pin hopes on the newer drugs. When Risperdal came along, it worked far better than any previous medication with fewer side effects. And now Zyprexa is proving even more miraculous. I know there will be others.

Of course I may simply be seeing a changing personality. Elene has been many different people through the years. True, we all play varying roles in life; I was not the same person when lecturing as I was at home. Behind the lectern I felt myself opening up into a knowing, confident, commanding and demanding master. I seldom was that person in other situations. My seven-year-old persona was hardly my seventy-seven-year-old persona. But through all the parts I have played and still play (worker, husband, lover, father, grandfather, or churchgoer), through all the years of cell growth and cell replacement, I retain an inner assurance of unity, a continuity binding all the transient selves. It is hard for me to imagine losing that identity.

I believe that on various occasions Elene has lost that core of herself. She has become someone else, willingly or not. This is not to say I felt she was subject to multiple personalities, a common misconception about schizophrenia. It was simply that her personality changed dramatically from time to time. When she would not let us touch her or hug her, I felt that someone else had moved into that body. There are whole years of her life that she now contends she can't recall, though her memory is keen for the surrounding times. Sometimes she talks as if she lost herself with the loss of Micah. Sometimes parts of her self, like the sense of smell, have been destroyed, notably with the cutting of her pubic hair. Often her self has been imposed on by forces that she fears—doctors, rays, auras—and she has consequently been unable to act or feel as she once did. Sam Wurlitz seriously considered taping Elene's episodes to play to her later, partly to convince her that she was ill and needed help, but more to the point here, to face the problem of her own identity, to demonstrate the different person who emerges when she is really troubled.

I make no claim to understanding the self, but does it not seem that to maintain an intact self one needs familiar people off whom to bounce that self? Don't we only know ourselves in relation to others we know or love? If so, then I could be right in feeling that when Elene was denying us and forgetting her boys (as when she wandered homeless), she had lost or buried her true self and some other self had taken its place.

Shirley and I never ceased wondering if the marriage of Elene and Karma was the right thing for her. Although the two held some harmonious obsessions like vegetarianism and ecological concerns and even spirituality, in many ways they were galaxies apart. He smoked. He had little background in art or classical music. He welcomed technology. He watched as much TV as his boys. He reveled in computer games. He owned every telephone gadget and subscribed to every mechanized service available. For him the only problem with technology was its cost, and somehow he found ways to finesse that.

Far more important in their relationship as I saw it was the absence of little acts of thoughtfulness and caring. Jill Ker Conway tells of her husband's psychological bouts with deep manic depression. She, however, remained close with him, sympathizing, caring, and searching for understanding. To combat Virginia Woolf's spells of schizophrenia, her husband provided good housing, regular food, medical attention, and endless support.

For many reasons beyond his control Karma seldom was able to provide such things for Elene. Instead of supporting her, he argued with her or became violent. When exasperated, he put her out of the house. Probably without thinking, he would let her walk from their house on a dark country road for a couple of miles to catch the bus on Highway 9 down to Santa Cruz and her room in the satellite house.

These are mere shades of difference, for with any kind of husband, Elene would have had troubles. And she always claimed to love Karma, even when he put her out of the house. She had an excuse for every one of his idiosyncrasies. She flew at us whenever we said anything disparaging about him.

And before I level any judgments on Karma, how about us? Elene might well, too, have done better with different parents. With all her boundless love, Shirley was often on a different wavelength. Instead of reprimanding or arguing, Shirley intuitively wanted to retreat into silence, to stop talking, to leave the room. That sometimes alienated Elene, because her natural response was Niagaras of talk that required someone to stand and listen. Each of those approaches irritated and exasperated the other.

And looking back, I can see how seldom I provided the force and the certainty that might have helped. I was far more likely to qualify, to want to know more before a conclusion, to act the scholar and historian. An authoritarian might have given Elene more support, more piers on which to build the bridges. Instead of taking a firm stand, I was more likely to see some merit in Elene's contrary positions, more often concluding that her basic insights were so sound that it was wrong for me to stifle them.

I represented as well the paradox of two disabilities facing one another. What effect did my developing blindness have on her stability? If the conformity to society's norms is the definition of sanity, my blindness was robbing Elene of any such model in me. In most people's minds a father should be strong, agile, provident, clear-sighted, and reliable. He should not be a groping, unsteady, cane-tapping, misty-eyed blind man. Her childhood effort at suicide may have been no more than a call for help, and one wag has said that the mentally ill are those whose noose broke, meaning they've all tried suicide. But the distinguishing aspect for Elene was her directive that her eyes be transplanted to mine, which at one level I might see as her effort to transform me into a normal father. Given some tendencies in the direction of trouble, could Elene have been pushed over the edge by my disability?

Then was the adoption agency correct, the one that turned us down as parents in 1954? Maybe, but the question is more general. Is permissive child rearing particularly dangerous when dealing with mental instability? Put that way, I suspect the answer is clear enough. But the question is not always that easily phrased. In Elene's young life we assumed that she was a gifted child, needing space and freedom more than discipline. And once mental illness emerged as a possibility, rationalizations and excuses followed. There were many times when I could think of Elene as impractical, unreasonable, even eccentric, but in those days I could never think of her as defective. Her idiosyncrasies were those of her adolescence and her times. She was little different from hundreds of kids in her generation, or so we could reason.

Indeed I often thought that her originality and freedom from conventionality allowed her to see more clearly than we who were more intimately engaged with the world. Perhaps the romantic, like me, who finds reason as only a partial guide in living, does not make the best parent.

Our friends sometimes gave the impression that they believed Elene was a spoiled child and we were too indulgent. But Elene's rages never seemed to us those of a spoiled child. A spoiled child is one who has learned to manipulate the parents. I suspect that Elene more likely felt that her parents manipulated her. Children who feel that their parents are manipulators often burst out in murderous rage. Could Elene deep down have held similar feelings? She did accuse me once of using height to throw my weight around. In her thinking, perhaps we had manipulated her by not providing her the chance to find another place in the sun, another community, another country. Instead we repeatedly claimed that Santa Cruz with its unusually helpful mental health services was the right place for her to be. To me that was no more than a father trying to orient the world as a protection for his child. But was it also the seed of manipulation?

We have been helpless to protect her from periods of homelessness. By selling our big house and moving to a retirement community, we had withdrawn one retreat for her. We had in short not protected her from herself. These, too, could have been the subtle ingredients of concealed, sublimated anger. And as Joanne Greenberg says in *I Never Promised You a Rose Garden*, the ground of mental illness is a "malignant and pernicious loneliness," which our removal of a retreat for her probably didn't help.

Professor Torrey warns that Greenberg mistakenly represents schizophrenia, but at least she is talking about mental illness. And, incidentally, she adds "boredom" as another symptom. I cannot say that I ever thought Elene suffered from boredom. Loneliness, yes, but not boredom. Perhaps her upbeat nature protected her from boredom.

Most modern theories relieve parents of being agents or causal factors in schizophrenia. But one concept says that unusually effective parenting can often minimize or fend off schizophrenia. Maybe we simply were not unusual enough. But then I must return to the advice of every professional around, that parenting has little or nothing to do with mental illness, except possibly in the genetic sense. Recent MRIs show that schizophrenic brains are unlike others, which must suggest that nature trumps nurture. But that is far from saying that parenting and the environment are unimportant.

I am aware that parents can be absolved from responsibility if we assume that a gene or an interaction of genes cause schizophrenia. Yet studies cloud that possibility, since an identical twin has only a 28 percent chance of developing the twin sibling's illness, and if it is genetic, how do we explain the heavy predominance of winter and spring births of schizophrenics? The same goes for chemical imbalance, like the excess of dopamine in the brain. If such is named the cause, what caused the change in the quantity of dopamine? Proof of direct genetic or chemical cause may yet come, but we don't have it yet. I like far better the theory that genetics is a predisposing, not a determining, factor. And in that case, though the predisposition may be there, parenting, environment, stress, infections, medications, vitamins—all of these factors may put parenting back into the picture.

In the 1960s R. D. Laing did a study of eleven British families of schizophrenic women. I couldn't find myself relating to any of them, but the study did teach me one thing—that what the parent sees in any situation may likely be viewed by the child in a completely different light. I know that if Elene were writing this book, it would hardly be the same. When I talk with her about those six months we spent in England, she speaks of them as a high point in her life, while to Shirley and me they were filled with frustrations and worries about her. The months of her later homelessness left us agonized while they probably for her were filled with rewarding experiences. I hope readers understand that this book is a record of my feelings and not those of Elene.

For parents, nevertheless, generalizations about child rearing inevitably turn inward. The psychoanalyst Carl Goldberg tells of a cold-hearted war criminal who abruptly terminated psychotherapy with a ringing accusation:

You are not superior to me. You just haven't been tested. I've been alone and terribly afraid all my life. I've been to hell and forced to follow the orders of devils. What would you have done in my place? No better than me, I'll bet.

There is truth there. I have never been tested as Elene has been. I have never lived in loneliness and fear, banished to any dark wilderness or singed by the intense fire of my perceived truth. I have never felt my inner self to be unrelated to what was going on outside. I have not been forced to follow the orders of devils. Hence my take on this story can never be the same as Elene's.

Not long ago I saw a ranting, mentally disturbed woman on the street with a police car approaching. I prayed that the police would be kind and gentle and treat her with respect. I couldn't forget the few times in desperation I have called the police on my own daughter. Of course, I rationalize. It was never a call for incarceration, but rather an appeal for physical assistance or a cry for treatment. But rationalization does not automatically include forgetting or forgiving oneself.

Shirley and I always loved Elene deeply, and never for a moment in our minds did we abandon her. But how many times did we feel frustrated in finding simple ways to help her? I have read that it took Jill Conway three years to understand how to care for her mentally disturbed husband. It has taken me forty, and I'm not sure I'm there yet.

Probably in the long run, the ones who will truly protect Elene will be Gale and Jonathan. I saw it already happening when Elene was entering her forties and the boys their teens. I felt they were even then providing a central direction, a comforting compass. In times of her deepest despair, I could see the way her face would light up at a story of Gale or Jonathan. Elene has come to accept their judgments on clothes and food and activities. I have seen them take her hand when needed, tell her it's time to go, convincing her to do what is required. Love flows between the three of them like a natural vapor, not superficially evident but as pervasive as air itself. Is love enough? Of course not, any more than being good is enough to disperse the evil in the world. But love, "like break of day from sullen earth arising," is the source of support, and support is the light that can surround and bathe, if not defeat, the tyranny of illness.